YOUR SUBCONSCIOUS MIND

DR. TAMERAT WORDE GEBREKIDANE

BALBOA.PRESS
A DIVISION OF HAY HOUSE

Balboa Press books may be ordered through booksellers or by contacting:

Balboa Press
A Division of Hay House
1663 Liberty Drive
Bloomington, IN 47403
www.balboapress.com.au
1 (877) 407-4847

Because of the dynamic nature of the Internet, any web addresses or
links contained in this book may have changed since publication and
may no longer be valid. The views expressed in this work are solely those
of the author and do not necessarily reflect the views of the publisher,
and the publisher hereby disclaims any responsibility for them.

The author of this book does not dispense medical advice or prescribe
the use of any technique as a form of treatment for physical, emotional,
or medical problems without the advice of a physician, either directly
or indirectly. The intent of the author is only to offer information
of a general nature to help you in your quest for emotional and
spiritual well-being. In the event you use any of the information in
this book for yourself, which is your constitutional right, the author
and the publisher assume no responsibility for your actions.

Any people depicted in stock imagery provided by Getty Images are
models, and such images are being used for illustrative purposes only.
Certain stock imagery © Getty Images.

Print information available on the last page.

ISBN: 978-1-5043-2123-5 (sc)
ISBN: 978-1-5043-2124-2 (e)

Balboa Press rev. date: 03/26/2020

CONTENTS

1

YOU'RE SUBCONSCIOUS MIND FOR HOME

Y OU ARE DOING WHAT YOU are doing, you are to be focused what you are doing in your home or you are distracted by your subconscious mind. When you are starting what you are doing you cannot be stay into what you have a mindset.

You are easily to move into a different mindset, what you have a mindset to be your subconscious process. When you are conscious what you are conscious your subconscious mind you cannot to do, what you want to do in your home.

You are not too congruent for your intention, when you are to live into what you have intention, you are to be servant for your subconscious mind, you are to be competent in your conscious mind and subconscious mind for your subconscious programming.

When you are competent for your subconscious

programming, you are not to focus for what you want to do in your home because you are to live easily different mindset, when you are living, what you are living, you can not to move into what you want to have, what you are congruent mindset to be your subconscious programming.

When you are to be keeping what you are keeping mindset, you can to get what you have now, you are not enjoy by what you have because, the mindset cannot to give, what you want to have, you cannot to change what you have a emotional reality, you have more what you have a reality.

When you are thinking from what you have a mindset, you can to gain more what you have emotion reality, to have, what you want to have, and you have to be living into what you want to do home. To do that, you have to competent your right mindset instead of your subconscious mind.

When you are competent for your right mindset that what you want to do in your home, you can to change what you have a reality because, you are conscious in your conscious mind to be not your subconscious programming.

You are to live, to be in your conscious mind, to be your right mindset that what you want to do in your home, when you are competent in your conscious mind, you are to move into what you want to have because you are conscious to be in your conscious mind your right mindset, when you are keeping what you are keeping the right mindset you are to change what you have a reality and to have what you want to have in your home.

Your subconscious mind help you for your home, to be enjoy, or, you can to have, what you have a mindset that you are bring from your brother, you are to be thinking, what you are thinking that you are bring from your brother, you are, to have your brother mindset, what he has a mindset to be angry.

You are not to keep, what you have enjoy mindset, you are conscious to be in your conscious mind your subconscious reaction, you are to keep thinking from what you have a mindset, when you are to be keeping what you are thinking, you can to have the wrong emotion because you are to live into the wrong mindset.

What you have a mindset that it comes from your subconscious mind, when you have, what you have emotion, you can to get hurt from what you have a mindset, you are to victim from your subconscious mind.

Your subconscious mind not help you, to have a good mindset, if you are every day to be condition what you are condition and to have, what you have, you are a victim of your subconscious mind, when you are victim of your subconscious mind, you can to have more what you have emotion that not to give, enjoy life in your home.

If you want to be enjoy in your home, you have to have the right mindset, not living into your right mindset and to live into your subconscious programming mindset, you can to be bring, what you are bring mindset.

This mindset can to give more what you have a wrong emotion, you are focusing in your conscious mind what you have a mind, when you are keeping what you are congruent mindset, you can not to change your reality.

To change what you have a reality, you have to be living your right mindset, to live into your right mindset, you need to detached, what you have mindset that the wrong mindset, when you are detached from your subconscious programming mindset.

You are now to focus into your right mindset, you can to start vibrate differently, what you are vibrate not to be what you were vibrate, you have a different vibration, this you have a vibration, coming from what you have a mindset, when you are living most of time in your right mindset you can to bring your enjoyment in your home.

Your subconscious mind to bring, what you have a procrastination mindset in your home, when you are home, you want to do thing but you can to move a different mindset, you have, what you have a procrastination mindset.

When you have, what you have a mindset, you are to be thinking from what you have a mindset, to bring, to be procrastinated into what you want to do. You have a subconscious mind that not to help you, to do, what you want to do, it puts you, to have the wrong mindset.

If you are keeping, what you are keeping, that what you have a mindset you cannot to do, what you want to do, you are misaligned the right mindset, you are aligned, what you are aligned mindset, this you are aligned, to give you, to be procrastination from what you want.

You are to be victim from your subconscious mind, when you are victim from your subconscious mind, you are to choice your subconscious programming that to give, to be procrastinated, you are living wrong mindset, you can to have more, what you have a wrong mindset.

You can not to move into what you want to have in your home, you are living most of time in the wrong mindset, if you want to move, what you want to have, you have to be

4

living the right mindset, to live, your right mindset, you have to be greater than your subconscious mind.

When you are greater than your subconscious mind, you are to starting to choice, you want to do in your home instead of to choice your subconscious mind programming, what you are choice, to be now, what you want to do home, and you are focusing the right mindset.

You can to start to change, what you have reality in your home, what you are conscious to be in your conscious mind, to have a different mindset, this you have a mindset, to be, what you want to do home, you are now, to be moving into what you want to have, you have the right mindset, this you have a mindset, to magnetized what you want to have in your home.

You are distracted by your subconscious mind in your home, you have missed your happy mindset because of by having what you have a mindset. When you have, what you have mindset, you can to lose your energy. You have a mindset, to bring, what you are bring energy that not to give a happy moment in your home.

You are, to living your subconscious programming, when you are keeping what you are keeping mindset, you can not to change, what you have energy. What you have a mindset, to be, you're wrong mindset that you are bring from your subconscious mind, you are to be, victim of your subconscious mind.

What you have intent to be your subconscious programming, when you are congruent into what you are congruent mindset that it comes from what you have intent, you can to have, what you have energy level that not to give you happy life in your home, what you have a mindset, can to be create, what you have wrong energy level.

If you are keeping, what you are keeping that it means, you are congruent what you have a mindset, when you are living, by what you have a mindset, you can not to change, what you have energy reality, you are, to be, to keep, what you have energy level in your home.

If you want to be happy in your home, you have to have the right mindset, when you are not to be distract by your subconscious mind, you are to focus in your conscious mind your right mindset, you can not to get, what you are getting before energy level, you are now to congruent your right mindset.

When you are, to be keeping, what you are congruent mindset, you can be bounce back quickly your happy moment in your home, you are, to live your right mindset, you are not to vibrate like what you were vibrate, you have a different vibration, what you have vibration to attract what you have a happy moment in your home, you are no longer to be victim by your subconscious programming because you are now living into your right mindset.

Your subconscious minds help you, to do what you want to do in your home, when you are doing what you are doing in your home, you are, to be live in a different mindset, when you are doing what you are doing because you are condition to be something and to have what you have a wrong mindset.

When you are living by what you are living mindset, you can to have, what you have feeling because you are to focus in your conscious mind, what you are condition that it comes from your subconscious mind. When you are focusing, what you are focusing in your conscious mind, to focus, what you are focus your subconscious reflection from the condition that to be wrong mindset.

You can to keep, what you are keeping mindset this you have a mindset can to give you, to have more what you are feeling. You cannot to do in your home what you want to do, you are conscious the wrong mindset, when are focus what you have a mindset, you can not to change the reality.

You are congruent what you are congruent mindset that your wrong subconscious programming. When you are congruent what you are congruent mindset, you are, to be, keeping what you have a reality, you are to vibrate, what you are vibrate from what you have a wrong mindset that to attract what you are attracting.

To do, what you want to do in your home, you have to have the right mindset, not living into your right mindset, you can to keep what you have reality, to change what you have a reality, you need to be live your right mindset, to live your right mindset, you need focus into what you have a mindset that your right mindset. When are keeping focus most of time in your right mindset, you can not to be active, what you were active feeling, you are in a different mindset that your right mindset that to change your reality.

Your subconscious mind is, to create in your home a negative mindset, when you are reading a book. You do not to get, what you have a state of mind before because you are living in the negative mind that it comes after you finished the conversation call.

When you have, what you have a mindset, you can not to focus, what you want to focus, you have a mindset to be your subconscious mind process. You are thinking from what you are thinking mindset to generate more negative energy.

You are too congruent the negative mindset, when you are keeping conscious in your conscious mind, what you have a negative mindset, you are to be, feeding your energy for the wrong mindset that to bring more a negative energy.

You are to be, victim your subconscious mind, because you are living your negative mindset that it is coming after you finished your phone conversation, you are not living, what you were living mindset in your home, what you have a mindset to be a different mindset.

If you are keeping what you are keeping a negative mindset, you are, to be, resisting into what you had a mindset, when you are living, what you are resisting mindset, you can to be, to live what you are living energy that to give you more negative energy.

If you want to be, bounce back quickly, you need to move from what you have a mindset, not moving from what you have a mindset, you cannot to get bounce back quickly. To get bounce back quickly, you need to live into your right mindset.

To live your right mindset, you have to be greater than what you have a mindset, but having a resistance mindset, you can not to move into what you want to have, what you have a mindset to be your resisting mindset. You can to keep what you have a negative energy.

When you are to be greater from what you have a mindset, you are not focus your wrong mindset. You are now living in your right mindset, what you are focusing in your right mindset; you can to change your energy level.

YOUR SUBCONSCIOUS MIND

Because you are focusing in your right mindset that it is bringing the right energy level, you are now to read your reading in your home happily.

Your subconscious mind can to give you, what you have a mindset, when you are watching tv in your home. You have not to have, what you have a good mindset before. You are living in your subconscious mind that you are bringing from watching tv.

When you are conscious in your conscious mind that your wrong mindset. You can to resist your right mindset, you are talking about what you have a mindset, you are congruent into your wrong mindset, this you have a mindset can to give what you have a feeling in your home that you do not want to have a feeling.

If you are unconscious your mindset, you can to keep, what you have a resisting believe in your right mindset. You are not, to be competence in your conscious mind, because you are to live most of time in your conscious mind your wrong mindset that to give you, what you have a wrong feeling.

If you live, by what you have a mindset, you cannot to change what you have a feeling reality. You are congruent the wrong mindset that not to give what you want to have a feeling in your home. If you want to change what you have a reality, you have to change what you have a mindset.

Not to change what you have a mindset, you can to keep, what you have a pattern that it comes from what you have a mindset, if you are keeping, to active what you are active pattern that to bring, what you have the same feeling, you can, to be bored in your home because you are a victim of your subconscious mind.

If you want to get, what you want to get in your home, you have to live your right mindset, not knowing your right mindset and living into what you have a mindset, you can not, to change your reality because what you have a wrong mindset can to give only what you have now.

So, you need to be moved from what you have a mindset, if you want to have a reality change, when you are moving into your right mindset, you cannot to activating, what you are activating pattern, you are living in a different mindset that what you have a mindset to be your right mindset.

When you have in your conscious mind your right mindset, you can to vibrated, what you are vibrating that to attract what you have a feeling that what you want to have a feeling in your home. If you are living most of your time into what you have a mindset? You cannot to bore in your home, what you have a mindset to give, what you are feeling that to bring a great life in your home.

Your subconscious mind distracted you not to have fun in your home, you have had the wrong mindset that from your subconscious mind. What you are memorized mindset, to be blame mindset, you have in your conscious mind. You are saying, why he did that for me, he is wrong, I am not expected and others. You are to drain your energy because you are living into the wrong mindset.

When you are living in your blame mindset, you can to vibrate, what you are vibrating, to keep your energy to drain. You are congruent what you have a mindset, when you are congruent, what you are congruent. You are, to be not to change, what you have energy level.

You cannot, to have a fun from what you have a

mindset, you are incongruent from your right mindset. You are not to change, what you have energy reality because you are to be keeping the wrong mindset. When you are living, what you are living that your blame mindset you can to have what you have feeling.

You are victim of your subconscious mind, what you are conscious in your conscious mind to be your subconscious process that blames mindset. You cannot to expected from what you have a wrong mindset to have fun in your home. You are living in the wrong mindset that not to give fun in your home.

So, you need to change, what you have a mindset. If you want to have, what you want to have mindset, not changing what you have a mindset. You are, to be keeping what you have emotional and thought reality. You are to gain more from what you have a mindset, what you have thought and feeling

But, living in your right mindset, you can to start to change what you have a thought and feeling. You are conscious in your conscious mind your right mindset that to magnetized the right emotion that to give you fun in your home. When you are keeping your right mindset, you cannot to active, what you were activating energy. What you have energy different that it comes from your right mindset, to give you fun in your home.

Your subconscious mind helps you to do what you want to do in your home. You are not staying into what you are doing because you have a text from your friend. You are, to think about what you have a message. You have, what you have a mindset to be the wrong mindset.

You can not to control your subconscious mind process.

You are to be into your subconscious process that what you have a wrong mindset. When you are contemplated from what you have a mindset, you can be to magnetize a different felling that it is not to give a relaxed moment in your home.

You are in the wrong state of being, you can to have a different thought, you are sticking into what you have a mindset, you can be generated the wrong thought that to lead in your home to have the worst day, you are bored by what you have a state of being.

You are victims of your subconscious mind, what you have a mindset in your conscious mind to be your wrong mindset. You cannot to change your energy level because you are living into what you have a mindset. When you have, what you have a mindset that your wrong mindset, you can to active, what you are activating the wrong emotion.

You are conscious in your conscious mind, is your subconscious mind process. When you are keeping, what you are keeping in your conscious mind, you cannot, to change your reality because you are staying in the wrong mindset that to give you, to have what you have a reality.

If you want to change what you have emotional reality, you have to be change, what you have a mindset. when you are moving into your right mindset, you cannot to get bored in your home, what you have the right mindset to have a different vibration that to generated what you want to have in your home that to be enjoying.

Your subconscious mind not helps you, when you are reading a book. Because you were hearing a music that you are condition to be the music, to bring the wrong mindset. You cannot to focus into what you are reading. You are focusing in the wrong mindset that what you are condition mindset.

When you are focusing, what you are focusing, you are just to see, what you did. You said, I am wrong, how I can think in that way and so on. You are unconscious in your conscious mind, when you do, what you do behavior in your home. You have not, to be reading moment. You are conscious, to be, is your subconscious programming.

You do not to have a good moment in your home. What you have a mindset can not to give you, what you want, is a reading moment in your home. You are to be living in the wrong mindset, when you live in the wrong mindset, you can not to change what you have a reality.

Because, you are conscious in your conscious mind is your wrong mindset. When you are conscious, what you are conscious in your conscious mind to be your wrong mind, you can be too active, what you were activating mindset that to lead, to keep what you have emotional reality.

You are victims of your subconscious mind, because you are processing an automatically from subconscious mind to be the wrong mindset. When you are keeping, to be focus in your conscious mind, what you have a wrong mindset, you cannot to be, to change, what you have an energy level. You are condition into your subconscious mind that to give more what you have now.

So, you need to be break, what you have a mindset, if you want to have changed. But, living in the wrong mindset and expected to have a different reality is impossible because what you have a wrong mindset can give only what you have emotional reality.

But, moving into your right mindset, you can not to get, what were getting before. You are living in a different mindset that what you want to have a mindset. This you have a mindset is not too vibrated like what you had a mindset. What you have a mindset is what you want to have a mindset, to have a different vibration that to give you a good feeling. When you have, what you have a mindset, you can easily to read in your home.

2

YOUR SUBCONSCIOUS MIND FOR YOUR EDUCATION

YOUR SUBCONSCIOUS MIND HELPS YOU to get, what you want to get in your education. You are bring your wrong mindset, you want to study but you have a wrong mindset that you are bring when were in the market, to be active the wrong mindset because your subconscious mind to process in the negative way from the condition.

You are living still in your subconscious process mind, when you are conscious in your conscious mind is your subconscious mind programming, you are not to get a good result in your education, you can not to focus in your education, what you are focusing to be wrong mindset.

When you are congruent, what you are congruent mindset, you can to active what you are activating. You cannot to change, what you are vibrating because you are focusing in your conscious mind to be your wrong mindset.

This you have a mindset to give what you have a vibration that to attract what you are attracting.

You are a victim of your subconscious mind because you are processing from your subconscious mind to be negative that you are living in your conscious mind is your subconscious process. You can not to change, what you have energy reality, what you have a mindset can to give only, what you have energy reality.

You are congruent the wrong mindset, when you are congruent, what you are congruent mindset, you can magnetized what you are magnetized energy reality. If you want to get result in your education, you have to live in the right mindset.

Not, living in your right mindset, you can to get, what you have result that to be the bad result .so, you have to move into your right mindset if you want to get, what you want to get for your education. When you are congruent into your right mindset, you cannot to have, what you had energy level, you are living in your right mindset that to bring the right energy level. You are now, can to study, what you want to study easily and to get result in your education.

Your subconscious mind can not to help you to do you're your education, you are conscious in your conscious mind is your subconscious memorizing. You are not to focus in your education. You are not congruent in your right mindset, you are, to be congruent the wrong mindset.

When you are conscious in your conscious mind is your memorized mindset. You can to active, what you are activating mindset this you have a mindset to give, what you have now. You are thinking from what you have a mindset this you have a mindset, to give you, to feel the way you are thinking.

You want to study but you are activating the wrong mindset, you do not to have a good energy level because what you have in your conscious mindset, to give you what you have energy level. When you are living into what you are living mindset, you can not to change what you have emotion reality.

When you are living, what you have a mindset to attract what you are attracting energy level. You are focusing in your conscious mind is your subconscious mind memorized. You are congruent into what you have a mindset that is your subconscious process.

You cannot to change your thought pattern from what you have a mindset. when you are keeping, to think from what you have a mindset you can not to change what you are feeling because you are focusing is your wrong mindset that can to be keeping what you have energy level. You are to be living most of time into your wrong mindset.

You are victims of your subconscious mind because you are processing from your subconscious mind to be the wrong and you are conscious in your conscious mind is your subconscious mind that to give you, what you have energy level.

You cannot to study from what you have a mindset, you needs to move into your right mindset if you want to change, what you have energy level but living into what you have a mindset; you cannot to be expected to have a different energy level. You are to attract, what you are attracting because you have, what you have pattern that is coming from what you have a wrong mindset.

If you want to get result in your education, you have to move from what you have a mindset. When you are moving from what you have a mindset and living the right mindset. You can to be change what you have energy level. When you are changing, what you have a wrong mindset and living in your right mindset you can to be study easily. You are to be competence in your conscious mind is your right mindset that to attract what you want to attract in your education.

Your subconscious mind to give you, to have what you have a doubt mindset. You are not congruent in what you want to have education mindset. You are living in your wrong mindset that to give a resisting into what you want to have a mindset.

What you are bringing from your subconscious mind is in your conscious mind. You are to be doubt, you said for yourself, I am too old, I cannot to get job, I cannot to afford and others. You are to keep what you have a mindset. You are sticking into what you have a mindset.

You cannot to change what you have a pattern, you are living into what you have a mindset. When you are contemplated from what you have a mindset, you can to have more what you have now. You are distracted by what you have a mindset not to have a good time in your moment.

When are keeping, what you are keeping that it means you are living in your wrong mindset. You cannot to change your pattern, you can to active, what you are activating mindset .you are focusing in your conscious mind is your subconscious process.

If you want to change, what you have a mindset. You have to live in your right mindset not living in your right mindset, you can to keep, what you are keeping that to bring what you have the wrong pattern. So you need to change, what you have a mindset and living your right mindset. You are to focus in your conscious mind your right mindset you can to magnetize what you want to have for your education.

Your subconscious minds not help you to have, what you want to have in your education. You are living into what you have a mindset that you are not to be peace with you, because you are seeing something that you are seeing to be in your conscious mind.

You are not being peace with yourself; you are to blame, you said, why I did that, which is not my fault and others. You are focusing into what you have a mindset, when you are to focus, what you are focusing, you are not to be peace with yourself.

You have not to have a good day; you are feeling to be sick because you are to raise your stress level .when you are keeping, what you are keeping a mindset. You cannot to change, what you have a chemical state. You are living in the wrong mindset that to keep what you have a chemical state.

You are victims of your subconscious mind. You are focusing in your conscious mind is your subconscious process that to give, what you have a mindset. When are living most of time in your wrong mindset you cannot to improved your feeling. You are, where you is to be your wrong mindset that to keep, giving what you have now.

If you want to get, what you want to get in your education. You have to live in your right mindset. When you have, what you have a mindset, you can not to be peace and you can not to change your chemical state. You are living in the wrong mindset that to give you, what you have now.

So, you need to live in your right mindset. To live your right mindset, you have to be break what you have a mindset but living into what you have a mindset, you are conscious in your conscious mind is your subconscious process that what you have in your conscious mind.

But, you are moving in your right mindset, you can not to have, what you had a chemical state. You are now living in your right mindset this you have a mindset to have a different vibration. When you are focusing in your conscious mind is your right mindset you are to be keep, what you have a vibration that to attract what you have a different attraction. When you are keeping, what you have a mindset. You are to be peace with yourself, you do not to have, what you had a thought and feeling. You are living in a different state of mind that is your right mind set. You are breaking what you had before and to magnetize what you want in your education.

Your subconscious minds not help you, to have what you want to have in your education. You have a day ritual of thinking, you are not focusing in your right mindset, and you are to be in your subconscious programming. What you have a psychic force to be in your wrong mindset.

When you are living, what you are living mindset, you

are to be wasted your energy and your time. What you are created a time in your mindset, to have your psychic force that to created, what you have a feeling in your mindset time line. You have the wrong frequency you have this you have a frequency is coming from what you have a mindset.

You are victims of your subconscious mind because you are bringing what you have a mindset from your subconscious mind. You are wanted to live in your subconscious mind. When you are want to be live in your subconscious, you are not to get what you want to have in your education. You have a different mindset this you have a mindset to be your subconscious ritual.

You can not to change your psychic force from what you have a mindset. You are still living in your conscious mind is your subconscious ritual, you have what you have a frequency that you have a frequency to magnetized what you have a thought and feeling.

If you are keeping what you are keeping mindset, you can not to change what you have an emotion reality. You are focusing in your wrong mindset, you can to keep what you have a vibration. You are not to move forward in your education, you are not to consume your energy and time.

You are backward for your education, you are fully focusing in the wrong mindset that to give what you have a time that you are not to enjoy. You are created what you have by what you have a mindset if you are willing to be unconscious in your mindset. You can not to be expected to change what you have a reality.

You are to be willing a victims of your subconscious mind, when you are willing, what you are willing a mindset, moving forward in your education to be impossible for you because you are sticking in the wrong mindset.

To break what you have, you have to move in the right mindset. When you are moving into your right mindset you can to start to change what you have a frequency because you are conscious in your conscious mind is your right mindset. Now, you can to start to move forward in your education because you are living into your right mindset that to gravitated what you want to have education.

Your subconscious minds help you to have what you want to have in your education or you are to be angry mindset that you have when are remember something, to process your subconscious mind to be angry. You are living in your conscious mind to be your angry mindset.

You do not to have a goodtime in your present moment, you are living in what you have a mindset. You are not good for yourself, you have not good thought about yourself, and you have a mindset to control you to have, what you have a thought and feeling.

You are a servant of what you have a mindset that is coming from your subconscious mind. You can not to control what you have a pattern, you are keeping saying, what you have angry about it; you are to feeling what you have a thought this is all doing by what you have a mindset.

You are unconscious in what you have a mindset, you are most time to live into what you have a mindset. When you are to live, what you are living mindset, you are incompetent, to live your right mindset in your conscious mind.

You are competent for your wrong mindset, to live in your conscious mind. When you are competent, what you are competent mindset that your wrong mindset, you can to active what you are activating. You are servant of your mindset, you can not to change, what you have energy level.

You are victims of your subconscious mind because you are living into your wrong mindset. What you have heaviness is coming from what you have a mindset. What you have not an easiness is coming from what you have a mindset, you are to be unconscious is your conscious mind. When you are unconscious your conscious mind, you are to be keeping what you have now. You are moving toward into what you have a wrong mindset that is brining what you have a life now. You are where you are because what you have a mindset not to give what you want to have education.

If you want to move toward into your education, you have to break, what you have a mindset. When you are breaking what you have a mindset and living in your right mindset you can not to active, what you were activating energy. You are now living in your right mindset this you have a mindset to create for you, to move forward into what you want to have in your education. Living most of your time in your right mindset to get what you want to for your education quickly.

Your subconscious minds not help you, to have what you want to have in your education. You are living in conscious mind is what you have a believe that to come from your subconscious mind, When you want to study, you are going to be in your believe system.

You can not to focus in your right mindset. You are to be in your wrong mindset, you said, my friend finished and not have a job, I do not have energy and other. You are a rat of your thought; you are keeping, to think from what you have a mindset.

When you are keeping, to think from what you have a mindset, you are to be overwhelmed by your thought, you can not to control your thought, what you have a mindset to produced, to have what you have a thought. You can not to have a fun, you are stressed by what you have a mindset.

You are to keep, what you have a mindset, you are to be unconscious for your mindset, you are under control of by what you have a mindset because you are conscious to be in your conscious mind is what you have a mindset.

You are a victims of your subconscious mind, what you have a mindset is coming from your subconscious mind. When you are living into what you have a mindset, you can not to be expected to have, what you want to have in your education. What you have a mindset can not to give what you want to have in your education.

You are moving backward for what you want to have in your education. You are congruent mindset is the wrong mindset. If you are focusing in your conscious mind, what you are focusing your wrong mindset you can not to change what you have an emotion reality.

You need to be congruent the right mindset but you are congruent in your wrong mindset, you can to keep, what you have energy level. To move forward into your education, you need to be living the right mindset. Living what you are living that it means you are in the wrong mindset that to keep you, to go backward into your education.

So, you need to live in your right mindset. If you want to move forward in your goal but living what you are living, you can to keep, what you have. How to move into the right mindset? You need to change what you have a mindset.

How to change my mindset? You have to know, what you are conscious in your conscious mind. When you know what you are conscious in your conscious mind, you are to start to change what you have now. You are conscious in your conscious mind is your right mindset; you can not to have, what you had before. You are living in your right mindset this you have a mindset to lead you into your direction that to move forward into your education.

Your subconscious mind to give you, what you have a mindset, you do not to have an attitude in your education. You are living in the wrong mindset, when you live in the wrong mindset; you can not to have a vibration pattern in your education.

You are in the wrong mindset, this you have a wrong mindset to vibrate, what you are vibrating. when you are holding on what you have a vibrate, you can to keep, what you have a traction that not to give, what you want to have in your education, you have a pattern of vibration to be your wrong mindset that only to give you, what you have now.

You are a victims of your subconscious mind because you are focusing in your conscious mind is your subconscious programming. If you are focusing in your wrong mindset that it means you have, what you have a mindset. You can not to change what you have a reality, what you have a vibration pattern is coming from what you have a wrong mindset.

You are to be willing a victim of your subconscious mind; you are most of time living into your wrong mindset.

You can not to control your subconscious programming; you are victims of your subconscious mind. You are unconscious in your subconscious programming that to give you, what you have a vibration pattern, you are conscious in your conscious mind is your subconscious programming.

When you are keeping, what you are keeping mindset that your wrong mindset, you can not to move forward into your education. You have a wrong mindset that to hold your education, you can to have, what you have a backward movement in your education; you have a wrong vibration pattern, you have.

If you want to achieved in your education, you have to change, what you have a mindset, what you have a mindset to give you always what you have attitude in your education. You are to be, where you are in your education, what you have a mindset, to hold you not moving forward in your education.

But, breaking what you have a mindset; you are not any longer to focus in your conscious mind. You are focusing in your conscious mind is your right mindset. When you are living in your right mindset, you can to change your vibration pattern, what you have a mindset not to have, what you have a vibration, you are in a different mindset that is your right mindset. When you are keeping your right mindset, you are to start, to move forward into your education, what you have a mindset to magnetized, what you want to have in your education. Living most of your time in your right mindset that your congruent mindset to have a vibration pattern in your education, you can to manifested quickly, what you want manifested in your education.

YOUR SUBCONSCIOUS MIND

Your subconscious minds not to help you, you are living in the wrong mindset that is coming from your subconscious mind; you are not to control your habit, when you want to study. You are to be going in your subconscious programming. When you have, what you have a mindset, you are too disconnected in your education, you are living in the wrong mindset, you are to be leak your energy. You are congruent into what you have a mindset.

When you are congruent, what you are congruent mindset, you are disconnected the right mindset. What you are congruent mindset to bring for you, not to do what you want to do in your education, resisting in your right mindset, not to move forward in your education and to staying where you are now.

You are victims of your subconscious mind, because you're subconscious to process what you have a mindset, when you are keeping into your wrong mindset, you are leaking energy, what you are conscious in your conscious mind is your wrong mindset.

You are to control, by what you have a mindset this you have a mindset is disconnected your right mindset, you are to waste your energy and your time, you can not to be move forward in your education, you are leaked your energy, what you have a time used by what you have a mindset.

If you are keeping control, by what you have a mindset? You are competence for your subconscious mind that is created what you have reality, you can not to have the right mindset in your conscious mind, you are most of time to have in your conscious mind is your subconscious programming.

You are to move backward in your education, because you are disconnected your right mindset, when you are disconcerted your right mindset, you have a wrong vibration pattern that it is coming from what you have a wrong mindset.

You are to be keep to leak your energy, what you have a mindset can not to give what you want to have; you are in the wrong mindset. You are to keep, what you have energy level, if you are living, what you have a mindset. You are congruent in your conscious mind is your wrong mindset. You can to active, what you are active energy.

If you want to move forward in your goal, you have to change what you have a vibration pattern. To keep, what you have a mindset, you are, to be willing to live in the wrong mindset that to disconnected from your right mindset.

You cannot to change, what you have a vibration pattern from what you have a mindset, what you have a mindset to vibrate, what you are vibrating, when you are vibrating, what you are a vibrating, you can to magnetized, what you are magnetized.

You are to keep, leaking your energy, so, you need to move into your right mindset, if you want to go forward in your education. When you are to start, to live in your conscious mind is your right mindset, you can to have the right pattern of vibration for your education that is bringing your right of emotion. You are now living in your right mindset you can to get, what you want to get in your education.

Your subconscious mind to give you, what you have a mindset because you are condition into the environment.

YOUR SUBCONSCIOUS MIND

What you have a mindset to be the wrong mindset, you are not to get, what you want to get that is your education.

You are not living in your right mindset, you are living in your subconscious process that is the wrong mindset, you are congruent into what you have a mindset. When you are congruent, what you are congruent, you are to be resisting in your education, and you cannot move toward into your education, you are staying, where you are now.

You are conscious in your conscious mind is your subconscious process. You are victims of your subconscious mind, you cannot to get, benefited from what you have a mindset for education. You are focusing in your conscious mind to be blaming someone.

You are thinking, what you are thinking from what you have a mindset that to created to feel the way you are thinking. You do not to have a good time because you are stressed by what you have a mindset. You are unconscious in your conscious mind is to keep what you have emotion that to give, to have more what you have a stress.

You are disconnected from your right mindset; you are to keep, to go backward for your education. You can to have from what you have a mindset is what you have a reality. You can not to change, what you have a reality from this mindsets, you have. You can to be created; from what you have a wrong mindset is what you have now.

If you want to have your education, you have to know your right mindset. Not knowing your right mindset is created not to have, what you want to have education. So, you need to be living into your right mindset. If you want to go forward in your education, when you are congruent into your right mindset, you can not to have, what you have a stressful life. You are in a different mindset that to be your right mindset. You are focusing in your conscious mind is your right mindset; you are to be move into what you want to have for your education.

3

YOUR SUBCONSCIOUS MIND FOR YOUR WIFE

YOUR SUBCONSCIOUS MIND IS NOT helping you, to have a good time with your wife. You have the wrong mindset when you have a conversation with her, you can to bring your subconscious process that you have now the wrong mindset. You are, to disturb yourself and your wife.

You have a disturb moment, you have, you do not have a good time with your wife, you are staying in your wrong mindset, when you are staying in your wrong mindset, you can to keep, what you have a mindset that to be a disturb moment.

You do not know, what you are disturb the moment, you are unconscious for what you have a mindset, you are just to focus in your conscious mind is your subconscious process for that situation. You are not to have from what you have a mindset to get a good time.

You are victims of your subconscious mind, you want to have a good moment with your wife but you have a disturb moment. You have a wrong mindset that to focus in your conscious mind, to keep what you have argue. You can not to have, what you want to have a moment form what you have a mindset.

You are congruent the wrong mindset, what you are congruent to give, what you have a now. You are unaware your wrong mindset, when you unaware your wrong mindset, you are to disturb from what you have a mindset, what you have a thought and feel not to give a good time.

You are not to go forward for good time with your wife, you are disconcerted form your right mindset. You are, to have, what you have disturb because you are living in your wrong mindset. If you want to have a good time with your wife, you have to live in your right mindset.

To live in your right mindset, you have to change what you have a mindset. If you are resisting in your wrong mindset, you cannot to have, what you want to have a time with your wife, you are to keep, what you are keeping that it is, to disturb yourself and wife.

So, you need to live in your right mindset, when you live in your right mindset, you cannot to have, what you have now, you are in a different state of being that is not to created what you are creating for yourself and your wife. You are now living in a different state of mind that is your right mindset. you are focusing in conscious mind is your right mindset, you are to change, how you feel for yourself and your wife, you have a good thought that to created a harmonized moment with your wife, you are going forward for relationship with your wife.

YOUR SUBCONSCIOUS MIND

Your subconscious minds help you, to have what you want to have relationship with your wife. You have, what you have a mindset, you are bringing from outside that you have in your home, you do not to have a good moment with your wife.

You are thinking, what you are thinking that from what you have a wrong mindset, when you live by what you have a mindset, you cannot to improved what you have a relationship, you are focusing in your conscious mind is your subconscious process.

You cannot to engaged with your wife probably, you have a time for what you have a mindset that to disturb yourself and your relationship. You are not to get, what you want to get relationship from what you have a mindset.

You are victims of your subconscious mind, you want to have a good relationship with your wife but you are unconscious is your conscious mind, when you are unconscious, what you have a mindset, you can to created what you have a reality.

You are living most of time to be in your wrong mindset, you can not to change, what you have emotion reality. If you want to have, what you want to have, you have to be living in your right mindset. What you have a wrong mindset, can to give you only what you have now that what you do not want to have a relationship with your wife.

If you want to improved, what you want to improve your relationship. You have to change, what you have a mindset, living into what you have a mindset help you to have, what you have a relationships. You are not to go forward for your relationship because you are stuck in the wrong mindset.

So, you need to be live in your right mindset, if you want to improve your relationship, when you are starting to live in your right mindset you cannot to have, what you have now. But to live in your right mindset, you have to know your right mindset, not knowing your right mindset and living in your wrong mindset, you can to improve your relationship.

When you know your right mindset, you are focusing in your conscious mind is your right mindset. When you are focusing in your conscious mind is your right mindset, you cannot to get, what you had before, you are living in your right mindset, you can to change what you have a relationship with your wife. You are now going into what you want to have a good time with your wife, what you have a mindset to magnetize what you want to have.

Your subconscious mind to give you, what you have a mindset, you have a good mindset, when you are talking with your wife but suddenly you can to have, what you have a mindset because someone invite her for lunch that she said to you, you have to live in your subconscious process.

You are in the wrong mindset, you do not want time to have with her, she asked you, to go somewhere for vacation with you but you have a resisting mindset, you have, you are conscious is in your conscious mind, what you are processing from your subconscious mind.

You do not to have a healthy feeling, what you are thinking from what you have a mindset to give you, what you are feeling, you are not going into what you want to have a time with your wife, you are disturb by what you have a mindset.

YOUR SUBCONSCIOUS MIND

When you are living most of your time into what you have a mindset, you can not to change, what you have a pattern for your wife, you can not to improved your relationship, you can not to have a good time, you can not to improve your healthy and others.

You are to be, where you are now. The mindset you have to have, what you have a pattern of thought that to created not to be harmonized, you are to keep not to be healthy, you are stressed by what you have a mindset. You are not control, what you have a mindset, the mindset you have is control you because you are most of time to live in your wrong mindset.

You are to be a victims of your subconscious mind because you have not too got, what you want to get from what you have a mindset, what you have a mindset to give you, not to be enjoy with your time, not to have a good time with your wife, not to have a healthy relationship and not to have a healthy feeling.

If you are living, what you are living mindset, you are still focusing in your conscious mind is your subconscious processes that not to change what you have a reality, you can not to be expected, to have a better relationship, better healthy feeling and better good time with your wife.

You are in the wrong state of mind, you are, when you are congruent in the wrong mindset, what you are congruent mindset to vibrate what you are vibrating, when you are vibrating, what you are vibrating, you are offering to have what you have.

To move into what you want to have a time for your wife, you need to live in the right mindset but living into what you are living, you can not to change what you have a feeling for your relationship, you are sticking, by what you have a mindset.

So, you need to live into your right mindset, if you want to change, what you have a reality. When you are moving into your right mindset, you can not to have, what you have, you are not to offer, what you are offering, you are in a different state of mind.

What you have a mindset to a have a different frequency because you are not conscious, what you are conscious in your conscious mind, you are conscious in your conscious mind is your right mind, when you are conscious, what you are conscious, you can to change your vibration, you can not to vibrate like what you are vibrating, what you are vibrate is your right mindset that to give you, what you want time with your wife.

Your subconscious mind not helps you to have, what you want to have time with your wife, you are living in the wrong mindset because you are lessening music, to remind you a previous wife. You are not too engaged with her properly. You are in your subconscious processes.

You are starting to compare your relationship, you are not to be happy by what you have a relationship, you are to blaming yourself for making the wrong decision. You are to disturb by what you have a mindset.

Your wife has to ask you, what she has wrong. But you are to be want to stay a time for what you have a mindset, you are thinking from what you have a mindset, when you are living into what you have a mindset, you can not to get, what you want to get a time with your wife.

You are now to be a victim of your subconscious mind, your subconscious mind is processing the wrong mindset, you are conscious in your conscious mind is your subconscious process, you can not to change, what you have a reality from what you have a mindset.

You are congruent in the wrong mindset, when you are congruent, what you are congruent, you can to have, what you have a pattern. You are not change what you have a thought and feeling, you are focusing in your conscious mind is what you have a mindset.

You are not to go forward into what you want to have a relationship; you are disturbing yourself and your wife by what you have a mindset. If are keeping, what you are keeping mindset, you are to be unconscious for what you have a mindset.

You are sticking the wrong mindset, you can to have more of what you have now that is to be, not to enjoy with your wife, not to enjoy with the relationship, not to get healthy life and other. What you have a mindset can always to offer you, to have, what you have a reality of life.

If you want to change, what you have, you have to live in the right mindset, when you are moving into your right mindset, you can not to have, what you have because when you are moving into your right mindset, you can to change what you have a pattern. When you change, what you are change, you can to have a good time with your wife, you are living in your right mindset, what you have a mindset to magnetized for your relationship.

Your subconscious minds not helps you, to have what you want to have a time with your wife. You are not to live your right mindset, you are distracted by your subconscious mind, and you are now living into the wrong mindset.

You are not too interested to have a time with your wife, you are want to focus into what you have a mindset. You are to be feed your energy into wrong mindset, you are to start, to strength your wrong mindset, when you are strengthening your wrong mindset, and you can not to have a good relationship with your wife.

You are disturb yourself by what you have a mindset, you are congruent the wrong mindset, this you are congruent mindset can not to give you, what you want to have a relationship with your wife, you are in the wrong mindset.

If you are living, what you are living mindset, you are conscious in your conscious mind is your wrong mindset. You can not to change the way you see for your relationship, you can not to change what you have attitude for your relationship, you can not to change how you feel about yourself.

You are sticking into what you have a mindset, you are not to go forward for your relationship, you are strength, what you have a mindset that to give more to have what you have. You are not to be breaking what you have a mindset; you are to keep, to disturb yourself.

When you live, what you live, you are disconnected the right mindset. You are to expected nothing from what you have a mindset that to have good relationship. If you are expected from what you have a mindset, you are unconscious, what you are conscious mindset. When you are unconscious for your wrong mindset, you are not to be aware the mindset that not to bring what you want to have a good time with your wife. You are most of time to live into your wrong mindset.

YOUR SUBCONSCIOUS MIND

You are victims of your subconscious mind because your subconscious is processing the wrong mindset; you are now living into the wrong mindset. When you are living, what you are living mindset you can not to change, what you have a reality.

If want to have, what you want to have a time for your wife, you have to break, what you have a mindset, when you are moving into your right mindset you cannot to experienced, what you were experienced. You are in a different sate of being that it is coming from your right mindset. When you are starting living in your right mindset, you are no strength the wrong mindset. You are now living not in the wrong mindset, you are now focus in your conscious mind is your right mindset.

When you are keeping, what you are keeping mindset, you can to have, what you want to have relationship for wife, what you have a mindset to be your right mindset, you are now to think different than what you were be. You have a different pattern, you have, what you have a pattern to strength your relationship. You are going, to have what you want to have a time with your wife, what you have a mindset to bring for you what you want to have.

Your subconscious minds not help you; you are in the wrong mindset because she is late coming home. You are to be live into what you have a mindset. You do not know what you are talking, you can not to control yourself, and you have not good words for her.

When you are living what you are living mindset, you can to change what you have a bad time, you can not to change what you have a feeling, you are in the wrong mindset what you have a mindset can to give you, to have what you have a relationship with your wife.

You are victims of your subconscious mind because you are now living into your wrong mindset. When you are living what you are living mindset, you can not to go forward to have a good relationship with your wife. What you have a mindset to strength what you have energy.

You are leak your energy, you are wasted your time and you are disturb yourself and your wife. You are conscious in your conscious mind is your subconscious processes that not to give, what you want to have a time with your wife. You are to keep what you are keeping because you are not living into your right mindset you are living in your wrong mindset.

If you want to change, what you have a reality, you have to know your right mindset, not knowing your right mindset and to live by what you have a mindset, you are to anchor your energy. When you are anchor your energy, you are to live what you are living reality that not to give you what you want to have a time.

You need to live into your right mindset, if you want to have what you want to have a time with your wife. When you live in your right mindset, you can to activate what you are activating. You are in a different sate that is coming from your right mindset. when are most of time to live into what you have a mindset, you are not to be anchor by what you had energy you are now living in your right mindset, you can to move into what you want to have a time for your wife, what you have a mindset to generated for what you want to have for your relationship.

Your subconscious mind not helps you, you have a

wrong mindset that you have is coming when you see your mother-in-law. You have a not a good word for wife, you are living in the wrong mindset, you are thinking form what you have a mindset.

When you are living, in the wrong mindset, you can not to get a good time. You are in the law energy level, what you have a mindset to give you a different perspective for your wife, your subconscious mind to give you, what you have a mindset, when you saw your mother-in-law.

You are disturb by what you have a mindset, you are not saying good thing for wife, you do not to have a good time, you are to be in what you have a mindset, you are not to lesson your wife word, you are living into what you have a mindset.

You are a victims of your subconscious mind, when you are living, what you are living, you are to be willing to stay in your conscious mind, when you are conscious, what you are conscious in your conscious mind is your subconscious process.

You can to be active, what you are activating energy. you said, I have a dark day, I am not happy by what I have a life, I am not enjoying by what I have a relationship, and others. You are not aware your mindset.

If you are living, what you have a mindset, you cannot to have a bright day, you are to keep what you are keeping, you are congruent the wrong mindset, when you are congruent, what you are you congruent mindset, you can not to change, what you have a bad day.

You are not going forward for your relationship; you are to go backward for what you want to have for your relationship. You need to break, what you have a mindset, if you want to have, what you want to have a relationship.

When you live in your right mindset, you cannot to have, what you have. To have what you want to have, you have to shift your focus, when you are focus in your right mindset, and you can not to have a low energy level. You are in a different state of mind that is your right mindset.

If you are living your right mindset, you can to move forward into what you want to have a relationship, because you are not to vibrate, what you are vibrating. You are now in your right mindset, this right mind set to bring for you, to have what you want to have a time with your wife.

Your subconscious mind not help you, you have not to have the right mindset, you have the wrong mindset because you are looking what she is a talking negatively, you have now a negative mindset that is coming from your subconscious mind.

Your subconscious mind is processing most of time negatively, when you have a time with your wife. You are competent to be for your subconscious mind, when you are competent in your conscious mind is your subconscious process.

You cannot to have what you want to have, what you have a mindset to created for you what you have a trapped life. You can not to change the heaviness of your life because you are in the wrong mindset. When you are living, what you are living mindset, you can not to get a good vibe of energy.

What you have a mindset to be a negative mindset, you can to vibrate differently, what you are vibrating to attract what you have energy, you have the heaviness of day, you have not to have a good attitude for your wife.

You are victims of your subconscious mind, you are not to get, what you want to get for your relationship. You are in the wrong mindset, when you are keeping your focus in your conscious mind is your wrong mindset, you can not to change, what you have a pattern of energy.

You want to have a good time but living the wrong mindset, you can not to expect to have what you want to have a good time. You are disturb by what you have a mindset, you are strength what you have energy level.

If you want to change what you have energy level, you have to know your right mindset, not knowing your right mindset and to live into what you have a mindset, you can not to change, what you have emotion, what you have a mindset can to give to have what you have energy reality.

But, to know your right mindset, you are not conscious in your conscious mind is your subconscious process. You are to live in your right mindset, you cannot to get what you had heaviness; you are now living in a different mindset that is your right mindset. When you live most of time in your right mindset, you can to start to break, what you have of emotion for your relationship. You are to brining, what you want to have a life for relationship, what you have a right mindset to magnetized for you.

4

YOUR SUBCONSCIOUS MIND FOR DAY TO DAY

YOU ARE NOT DOING WHAT you want to do today; you are living in a different mindset that you are bringing from your subconscious mind. When you live in to what you have a mindset that to be your wrong mindset. You are congruent the wrong mindset.

You cannot to do what you want to do. You are distracted by what you have a mindset, you are not engaged into what you want to do, you are conscious in your conscious mind is your subconscious mindset that not to give you what you want to have.

When you are living your today mindset that you have a wrong mindset can not to give what you want to get for your day, you are not too aware your right mindset. If you are not too aware your right mindset you cannot to get what you want to get for your day. You are living is the wrong mindset that to strength what you have a distraction of day.

You are victims of your subconscious mind what you have a mindset to have from your subconscious mind and to live in your conscious mind. You can not to move forward for your day what you have a mindset to take your energy and time.

If you want to have, what you want to have for your day. You have to know your right mindset, not knowing your right mindset and living into what you have a mindset you can not to improved, what you have a mindset cannot to give you improvement for your day. The mindset you have to give you, to be trapped in your day and to move backward for what you want to do for day.

To do what you want to do you need to have the right mindset, when you know your right mindset that you are to start the first step. To do what you want to do for your day, you have to congruent for your right mindset. You are now congruent the wrong mindset that you are congruent a mindset to created what you have a realty.

So, you need to live in your right mindset, if you want to do, what you want to do. When you are living in your right mindset you can not to have, what you have a reality. You are in a different state of mind that is your right mindset to vibrate is differently than what you were vibrate. When you are to focus in your conscious mind is your right mindset you can to start forward into your day plan.

Your subconscious mind not helps you; you are not doing what you want to do today. Your subconscious mind to reminded you by today date, you are living in your subconscious mind, what you have a mindset to be a negative mindset.

When you live into what you have a mindset, you can to have a healthy day, you are remembering something what you are remembered to bring for you to have what you have a feeling. You are thinking, from what you have mindsets, you said, he is stupid, that was the worst time, I was angry and others because you are living what you have a mindset.

You do not to have a good time today, you are disturb by what you have a mindset. You are living in the wrong mindset; you can not to go forward for what you want to do today. You are conscious in your conscious mind is your wrong mindset.

You are victims of your subconscious mind, your subconscious mind to process for you a negative mindset; you are to live in your subconscious process. When are keeping, what you are keeping mindset, you cannot to change, what you have a reality you are living in the wrong mindset.

If you want to do what you want to do today, you have to change what you have attitude for what you want to do today. Living into what you have a mindset to keep what you have attitude; you are not going forward you are to go backward for what you want to do today.

So, you need to move into your right mindset, if you want to go forward into your day plan. When you are changing what you are changing mindset and to move into your right mindset, you can not to have what you have a reality. You are now living different mindset that is your right mindset; you are living in your conscious mind most of time. When you are focus in your right mindset, you can to have what you want to have for your day that what you want to have for today.

Your subconscious mind not to help you, you are not to live into your right mindset. You have the wrong mindset that you have a mindset it comes when you meet your friend, you want to do something today but you are now living in a different mindset.

You are most of time to live into your wrong mindset. You do not have a time; to do what you want to do today you are with your friend you are not congruent with your right mindset, you are to move backward for today plan.

You are stressed out by your mindset; you have lost what you had a good mindset after you finished the conversation with your friend. You do not to have a good feeling for yourself, what you had been mindset to active what you have a feeling.

You are not conscious for you had a mindset with your friend, you had been most of time in the wrong mindset with your friend, you are now to live into what you had a mindset. When you live into what you have a mindset, you are not to live in your right mindset what you have now the wrong mindset.

You are victims of your subconscious mind; you are not to control your subconscious mind. You are to bring your subconscious process, you are now living in your conscious mind is your subconscious process, when you are living what you are living mindset you can not to change what you have a reality you are to be activate what you are activating reality from what you have a mindset.

You are wasted your time and energy because you

are focusing the wrong mindset, if you are keeping what you are focused mindset you are to feed your energy into what you have a mindset, you are to stuck into what you have a mindset.

You cannot to have what you want to have today, by what you have mindset if you want to get what you want to get for your day you have to know your right mindset, not knowing your right mindset and living in the wrong mindset you can not to get what you want to get.

So, you need to change what you have a mindset, if you want to have what you want to have, when you are starting to change your mindset. You are now living in your right mindset, what you are focus in your conscious mind is your right mindset. You are generated what you want to have for today what you have the right mindset to bring for you to have what you want to have today so, you need to stay in your right mindset.

Your subconscious mind to created a resisting, you are not living in your right mindset what you have a mindset is coming from your subconscious mind that to be your habitual way of thinking, when you are starting to live in your wrong mindset, you are not to get what you want to get today.

You are not congruent in your right mindset, what you have a mindset to be the wrong mindset. When you are thinking form what you have a mindset, what you have a mindset to give you, to be resisting into what you want to have today.

You are not to go forward into what you want to have today, you are in a different mindset that you have a wrong mindset to give you not to have what you want to have, you said, I will do tomorrow, I need to be rest, it is not a good day and others.

You are victims of your subconscious mind, what you have a mindset cannot too created what you want to have today when you live in your wrong mindset to strength your wrong mindset, you are to keep what you have a bad day for you.

You are control by what you have a mindset, what you have a bad to continue. You are going backward for what you want to have today, if you are keeping to live into what you have a mindset you cannot to change what you have a reality.

You are congruent the wrong mindset, this you are congruent mindset to keep your bad day. If you want to move forward into what you want to have today, you have to know your right mindset, not knowing and living in your subconscious process mindset that the subconscious process negative mindset you can to keep your victims of your subconscious process.

To go forward into what you want to have today. you need to be living into your right mindset, to live, you have to focus into your right mindset but you are to focus in your wrong mindset you are to feed your energy into the wrong mindset.

You cannot to change what you have energy level, you are still focus in your wrong mindset what you have a mindset cannot to change what you have energy level. You have to move a different mindset when you are moving in a different mindset you cannot to have what you have a bad day. what you have a mindset to be your right mindset, you are now living into your right mindset, you can to start to break a bad day and to have what you want to have today.

Your subconscious mind not to help you, you are not living in your right mindset, what you have a mindset to be your ritual mindset. You are now to live into your ritual mindset; you are not to be your right mindset, you are living what your subconscious process that you have a wrong mindset.

When you live, what you are living mindset you are to start to think from what you have a mindset. You are to worry about what you have a job, you are not to have a good thought from what you have a mindset, you are to active fight-to-flight, your heart to be working more, you are not to breath probably you are not to be enjoy what you have a moment, what you have a mindset to bring for you to have what you have now, you are not going forward for what you want to have today.

You are victims of your subconscious mind, your subconscious mind to process for you what you have, you are willing to have, what you have a mindset you are conscious in your conscious mind is your subconscious process, you are to going backward for what you want to have today.

If you are thinking, what you are thinking you can not to break what you have a stressful day, what you have a mindset can to give what you have now, you are congruent the wrong mindset. You are keeping what you are congruent mindset, you can to keep what you have a reality.

To move forward for what you want to have today, you need to live into the right mindset, not knowing your right mindset and to keep what you have a mindset, you are not to consumed your energy you are to be strength what you have a wrong mindset.

You are not to have a fun day; you are to be bored with your day. What you have a mindset cannot to change what you have a reality instead to give you more, what you have a stressful life, you can to keep what you have attitude.

To go forward into what you want to have today, you have to break what you have a reality. If you are living into what you have a wrong mindset you cannot to break your reality. To get what you want to get today, you need to be congruent your right mindset.

When you are congruent your right mindset, you cannot to have, what you have. What you have a mindset to be your right mindset. you can not to have what you had before, you are now living different mindset that is your right mindset, you are now to move forward into what you want to have today, what you have a mindset to magnetized for you, what you want to have today.

Your subconscious mind not help you, you are living in the wrong mindset because you are heard something when you are doing, what you want to do today. You are now living in the wrong mindset that it is coming from your subconscious mind.

You are changing your emotion set point; you are not doing what you are doing. You want to stay in your wrong mindset, when you keep it what you have a wrong mindset, you are not to be enjoy by what you have a moment; you are to be blame yourself.

You are victims of your subconscious mind, what you

have a mindset is coming from your subconscious process. You are focusing in your conscious mind is your subconscious process, you are not to be going forward for what you want to have today, you are living in the wrong mindset.

If you are most of time to live, you are to strength your wrong mindset and to keep what you have a disturb of day .when you are living in your wrong mindset, you cannot to change your emotional set point, what you have a mindset can to give what you have emotional set point.

If you want to move forward for what you want to have today, you have to live in your right mindset but living in your wrong mindset, you are to keep your backward to go in your today plan. What you have a mindset can not to change, what you have a reality.

To go forward into what you want to have today, you have to have the right mindset, living in your wrong mindset and expected to have what you want to have today, you can not to have what you want to have today from what you have a wrong mindset.

You need to focus into the right mindset; you are now focusing the wrong. If you are focusing, what you are focusing that your wrong mindset, you can not to change what you have a reality, you are still living in your wrong mindset. To get what you want to get today, it needs, to have the right mindset. When you have the right mindset in your conscious mind, you can not to have what you have reality.

You are focusing in your conscious mind is your right mindset, when you are focusing, what you are focusing mindset, you are to start to change what you had energy level, what you have a mindset not to bring what you had before reality instead of what you have a mindset to created for you, to go forward into what you want to have today. Living most of your time into your right mindset, you can to go moving fast into what you want to have today, you are living in a different mindset that you are most time living mindset is your right mindset.

Your subconscious minds not help you, you are not moving forward for what you want to have today. You are too excused into what you want to have a mindset, your subconscious mind is processed the wrong mindset that to give what you have a mindset.

You are not, to give your time into what you want to have today, you are not to give your energy into what you want to have today, you are to congruent the wrong mindset what you are congruent mindset to give you a resisting into what you want to have today.

You are victims of your subconscious mind because you are conscious in your conscious mind is your subconscious process, you are to going backward for what you want to have, you are now living the wrong mindset that not to give you, what you want to have today.

When you are living, what you are living mindset, you can to crated what you have a reality that not to give what you want to have. You have the wrong mindset, what you have a mindset to vibrate differently; when you are keeping what you are vibrating you are attracting what you are attracting.

If you want to move forward for what you want to have today, you have to know your right mindset, not knowing your right mindset can not to give what you want to have today. You need to congruent your right mindset if you want to get what you want to get.

If you are keeping what you are congruent mindset, you cannot to have what you want to have today. you are congruent the wrong mindset that you have a congruent mindset to offer you to have what you have now that you do not want to have today.

So, you need to break what you have a mindset, if you want to have what you want to have today. When you are break what you have a mindset and to move a different mindset, what you have a mindset is your right mindset.

You can not to have what you have a reality before; you are now living in a different mindset that you have a mindset is your right mindset. You have different vibration, what you have a vibration is not created what you had attraction.

What you have a vibration is to vibrated differently, when you are keeping what you are keeping mindset, you are to be keep what you have a vibration what you have a vibration to attract what you want to have emotion that what you want to have today. Living most of your time in your conscious mind is your right mindset; you are to keep what you want to have today.

Your subconscious minds not help you; you are not to live in your right mindset. You are to live into your subconscious process, when you want to do what you want to do today, you have what you have a mindset. You are feeding your energy, what you have mindsets to have strength because you give your energy into, what you have mindsets.

You are to sink down, you are not to be optimistic, what

you have a mindset cannot too created what you want to have today. You are not to moving forward for what you want to have today; you are living the wrong mindset that to give you more what you have now.

You are a victims of your subconscious mind, your subconscious mind is processing when you are doing what you are doing today is the wrong mindset. You are now living your wrong mindset, you are to sink down, and you are to move backward for what you want to have today.

You are not seeing a good thing form what you have a mindset, you do not have an optimistic word, you are tired by what you have a mindset, you have a big heaviness, you are to see, what you have seen of not to move forward for what you want to have today.

When you have, what you have a mindset, you can not to change what you have a reality. You are focusing in your conscious mind is your subconscious process that your subconscious mind to give the wrong mindset. You are now thinking from your conscious mind is your wrong mindset.

What you are thinking, not to give you what you want to have, you are congruent the wrong mindset. When you are congruent, what you are congruent you cannot to change what you have a thought pattern because you are living the wrong mindset.

If you want to be optimistic into what you want to have today, you have to know your right mindset, living into the wrong mindset to block what you want to have today and to keep sinking down by what you have a mindset.

To move forward for what you want to have today, you need to be living in your right mindset. When you are living into what you have a mindset, you can not to be expected to change what you have energy reality, what you have a mindset to strength what you have energy level.

If you want to break, what you have a mindset you need to change, what you have a mindset but living into what you have a mindset you can not to expected to have what you want to have today you are focusing in your conscious mind is your wrong mindset.

To get what you want to get today, you need to be congruent the right mindset. When you are congruent, what you are congruent is your right mindset, you can not to have, what you have a reality. You are now living a different mindset that what you have a mindset is your right mindset, living most of time in your right mindset, you can to move forward for what you want to have today.

Your subconscious minds not help you, you are not to live into your right mindset, and your subconscious mind defeated you. You are not to be your right mindset, what you have a mindset to be your subconscious mind process that you have now mindset.

What you have a mindset to said, you had been before but you had not to have, you are not good enough to have that, it takes long time to have what you want to have and others. You are too stuck in what you have a mindset.

Your subconscious mind defeated what you want to have today, you are conscious in your conscious mind is your subconscious process that your subconscious mind to give the wrong mindset. When you are conscious, what you are conscious mind is your wrong mindset, you can not to move forward for what you want to have today.

Your subconscious defeated what you want to have a mindset, when you are living, what you are living mindset;

you can to strength what you have a mindset that to go backward for what you want to have today. You are focusing the wrong mindset.

You are victims of your subconscious mind, you are living in your conscious mind most of time is your wrong mindset, when you live in your conscious mind, you can not to change what you have a reality, you are feeding your energy the wrong mindset that you have a mindset can to created for you, to have what you do not want to have today.

If you are keeping, what you have a mindset, you can to keep to go backward for what you want to have today. What you have a mindset can not to give you, what you want to want to have today. You are living in the wrong frequency.

To get what you want you want to get today, you have to defeated your subconscious mind. If your subconscious mind defeated you, you can not to change what you have a reality, what you have a mindset can to magnetized what you have now.

You have to change, what you have a mindset. When you change, what you have a mindset and to have a different mindset, what you have a mindset to be is your right mindset. You can not to have, what you have a reality, you are change your frequency what you have a frequency is coming from your right mindset. When you are living most of time in your right mindset, you can to move forward for what you want to have a mindset, what you have a mindset to magnetize what you want to have today.

5

YOUR SUBCONSCIOUS MIND FOR PAST LIFE

YOUR SUBCONSCIOUS MINDS NOT TO helps, you are not to live the right mindset what you have a mindset is coming when you see a photo, you are now to live in a different mindset, your subconscious mind is processing and to bring what you have a mindset.

You are not to control yourself, what you have a mindset to be in your conscious mind. You are thinking from what you have a mindset, to put you not to engaged in the moment, you are swept by what you have a mindset, you are to be upset by what you did something, you are freeze by what you have a mindset.

You are victims of your subconscious mind, your subconscious mind is processing what you have a mindset .when you have, what you have a mindset you cannot to be in the present, you are now living in your wrong mindset that you have a mindset to disturbed your present moment.

You cannot expect, to have what you want to have in your moment, you are living in the wrong mindset that your subconscious mind is processing when you see the photo, your subconscious mind is controlling you, you are to follow your mindset.

When you are to follow, what you have a mindset, you can to keep to disturb your moment, what you have a mindset cannot to give you enjoy moment, you are living in the wrong mindset. You are focusing in your conscious mind is your wrong mindset that not to give a good moment.

If you are keeping, what you are keeping mindset, you are to strength what you have a wrong mindset, you are under control of your wrong mindset that to knock of your day and to wasted your time. So, you need to be moving in your right mindset.

When you are moving in you right mindset, you can not to have, what you have a reality. To move into your right mindset, you have to break, what you have a mindset. Focusing on your conscious mind is your wrong mindset can not to change, what you have a reality.

To change what you have a reality, you need to focus your right mind. When you are focusing in a different mindset that you have a mindset is your right mindset, you can not to have, what you have before. You are now living in a different mindset, what you have a mindset to change what you had experience. You are now to have a different feeling in your present moment what you have a mindset to magnetized good thing for you.

Your subconscious minds help you; you are not living

in your right mindset, what you have a mindset t
from your memorized mindset that you have a mind
to give you the right mindset; you are not to do whc
want to do.

You are living in the wrong mindset, what you ha
mindset to bring your past life, you are to be upset by w
you have passed situation, you are looking from what y
have a mindset, to give you more stress.

You are not to move forward for what you want t
do, you are too conscious in your conscious mind is you
subconscious process, you are not to control, what you have
a mindset. What you are focusing in your conscious mind
is your wrong mindset.

You are victims of your subconscious mind ; you want
to do, what you want to do today but you are now living
in the wrong mindset, what you have a mindset to change
your state of being, you are congruent in what you have
a wrong mindset.

You are tired by what you have a mindset; what you
have a mindset to change your energy level, you are
unconscious of your mindset, you are still to keep what you
have a mindset. You are to move backward for what you
want to have today.

What you have a mindset can not to give you; what
you want to have, you are now living not your right mindset,
what you have a mindset is coming from your subconscious
process that you have a mindset to be a wrong mindset.

If you are keeping, what you are keeping mindset you
cannot to change, what you have a mindset. You are still
focusing in your conscious mind is your wrong mindset that

not to give what you want to have today, you are in the wrong frequency.

To get, what you want to get, you have to have the right mindset. Not knowing your right mindset, you can not to change what you have energy level, if you level by what you have a mindset to be pumping more stress that not to give a healthy life.

So, you need to be break; what you have a mindset, if you want to have, what you want to have today. When you are breaking; what you have a mindset you are not to get what you have an emotional reality, you are in a different mindset that you have a different mindset is your right mindset.

You are focusing in your conscious mind is your right mindset; you are not to vibrated like what you were vibrate, you are now living in a different mindset this you have a mindset to created what you have a vibration; when you are living most of time in your right mindset you are to move forward into what you want to have today

Your subconscious minds not to help you; you are bringing a different intention that when you are doing, what you are doing, your subconscious mind is processing a different intention. What you have intention to create a different mindset.

What you have a mindset to bring; what you have experience, that to give a resisting for what you want to do. You have been before for what you want to do today; you have a negative feeling, you have not to get, what you want to get at that time.

You want to do it now but your subconscious mind is processing what you have a mindset; you are now living in

your subconscious process mindset. When you have, what you have a mindset you are to be resisting in your want to do today mindset.

You are victims of your subconscious mind; you are to go backward for what you want to do mindset. What you have a mindset to strength what you have a reality; you are believe, what you have a wrong mindset, when you are believe, what you are believing mindset you cannot to change what you have a reality.

You are to go backward for what you want to do today; you are not living in the right mindset, what you have a mindset still your wrong mindset. You can not to change the way you see from what you have a mindset; you are still believe your wrong mindset.

You are focusing in your conscious mind is your wrong mindset; you are wasting your energy and your time in your wrong mindset, you are not to get, what you want to get from what you have a mindset. You are congruent the wrong mindset.

What you are congruent mindset to give you; to be resisting in what you want to do today, to be where you are and to believe what you have a wrong mindset. What you have a mindset to created the wrong vibration, when you give your focus into what you have a mindset to strength, what you have a mindset.

If you want to get forward for what you want to do; you have to break your resisting, not breaking what you have a resisting, you are to be keep what you have a mindset. When you live in your wrong mindset you can not to be expected to move forward for what you want to have today.

To move forward into what you want to do today; you need to know your right mindset, not knowing the right mindset, to keep what you have a reality that not to give, what you want to have a reality today. So, you need to know your right mindset.

When you know your right mindset; you are to start to move forward for what you want to do today, you have a different mindset this you have a mindset is your mindset, you are conscious in your conscious mind is your right mindset. You are focusing in your conscious mind is your right mindset; you are not to bring, what you bring vibration. What you are vibrating is your right vibration, when you are keeping what you are keeping vibration, you can not to attract, what you are attracting vibration. What you are attracting a reality is what you want to have today, Living most of time, to move fast toward into what to have today.

Your subconscious minds not help you; you are not to live in your right mindset, what you have a mindset to have when you see your old friend to process of a different mindset. What you have a mindset to change what you have feeling before.

You are not doing, what you are doing; you are in a different mindset this you have a mindset to activated anger. You are thinking from, what you have wrong mindsets; when you are thinking, from what you have mindsets, you are to change your breath, and you are to focus into your past life.

You are victims of your subconscious mind; you are not to move forward for what you want to do today. You are now living in the wrong mindset, you are focusing in your conscious mind is your subconscious process. When you are focusing, what you are focusing; you can to distribute yourself, what you have a mindset can not to give a good moment with your time.

If you are keeping, what you are keeping a mindset; you can to have what you have energy, what you have a mindset can not to change what you have energy, what you have a mindset not to give you for what you want to have today.

What you have a wrong mindset to strength what you have energy level; you are still conscious in your conscious mind is your subconscious process. When you are conscious, what you are conscious mindset is your wrong mindset, to keep your anger mindset that to bring for you a worst day.

To move forward into what you want to do today; you need to know your right mindset, not knowing your right mindset, you can to focus what you are focus mindset. You are too congruent the wrong mindset, when you are congruent what you are congruent to lose what you have before state of being.

If you want to go forward for what you want to have today; you have to change, what you have a mindset. When you are staying in your wrong mindset, you can not to be expected to move forward for what you want to do; you are not living in your right mindset, what you have a mindset can to magnetized what you have a reality.

You need to change, what you have a mindset ; if you want to have what you want to have today, to change what you have a mindset, you have to break your focus ; focusing into your wrong mindset you can to keep what you have a negative past life.

But, you are to change your focus ; what you have a mindset is a different mindset, you are to live your different mindset that you have a mindset is your right mindset, you are now focusing in your conscious mind is your right mindset, you are to start to change what you have reality, what you have a mindset is not creating what you have before, you are now living in your right mindset, what you have a mindset to bring what you want to have today.

Your subconscious mind not help you; you want to have a relationship but your subconscious mind is processing what you have a mindset, you have a mindset to be a different mindset you are now focusing into what you have a mindset.

When you are focusing, what you are focusing mindset you are bring what you have a past life relationship experience. You are comparing your relationship; you cannot see a good experience from what you have a relationship before.

You are victims of your subconscious mind; you are not go forward for what you want to have, you are living in the wrong mindset. When you are conscious, what you are conscious mindset in your conscious mind you are to bring what you have been a negative past life experience.

You can not to see good thing from what you have a mindset, you have a negative outlook into what you want to have a relationship, if you are keeping, what you are keeping a mindset you are to feed the energy for the wrong mindset you are leaking your energy and your time.

To get what you want to get relationship, you need to be living in a different mindset what you have a mindset can to created what you have a reality that what you have a reality to demagnetized what you want to have now, you are congruent the wrong mindset.

If you are keeping what you are congruent mindset; you are to disturb yourself, what you have a mindset can only to strength what you have a reality, what you have a mindset can not to give a good thought, when you are keeping what you are keeping thought you can to keep your distraction.

To move forward into what you want to have, you have to be living in the right mindset. You are not living in your right mindset now, what you have a mindset is a wrong mindset. When you believe what you have a mindset you can to keep backward for what you want to have.

To go forward for what you want to have, you need to find the right mindset but keeping what you are focusing in your conscious mind, to strength what you have a reality so; you need to be living in a different mindset.

When you are living in a different mindset you can not to have, what you have a reality. You live a different mindset that what you have a mindset is your right mindset; you are now focusing in your conscious mind is your right mindset, you are not to be focusing in your wrong mindset. You can to start to change what you have a reality, what you are focusing in your conscious mind is your right mindset to magnetized what you want to have a relationship.

Your subconscious minds not help you; someone said something about you, to process your subconscious mind and to give what you have a mindset. You are not living in your right mindset; you are now living in your wrong mindset.

You are to remember your past life, you are to

regretted by what you did you are now to bring what you had energy level ; you are not aware about when you are change, what you are changing your energy level you are focusing in your conscious mind is your wrong mindset.

You are victims of your subconscious mind; what you have a mindset not to give you what you want to have today, you are going backward for what you want to have today. You are conscious in your conscious mind is your subconscious process.

When you live, what you are living mindset you can to keep, to visited your past life by what you have a mindset. What´you are visiting by what you have a mindset; to be not to congruent in your right mindset, you are to bring the wrong energy and to be stacked in your wrong mindset.

When you are keeping, what you are keeping you are to strength what you have energy level. You are not to move forward for what you want to have today; you are still focusing your wrong mindset. When you are focusing what you are focusing you can not to change what you have a mindset.

To move forward into what you want to have today; you need to be break what you have a mindset, what you have a mindset can to give you, what you have a past a negative experience. If you are not aware your mindset you can to consume your energy into what you have a wrong mindset that to bring for you to have more what you have now.

So, you need to have a different mindset, to move forward for what you want to have today. When you are moving in a different mindset what you have a mindset is your right mindset, you are not to focus in your conscious mind is your wrong mindset.

What you are focusing in your conscious mind is your right mindset ; you can not to have what you have a reality, you are not living in your wrong mindset you are now living in your conscious mind is your right mindset, you can to move forward for what you want to have today. What you have a right mindset has a different frequency that to vibrate is differently than what you were vibrate; you are now to attracting what you want to have today.

Your subconscious minds not help you; you have a different mindset what you have a mindset is coming from your subconscious process; you are to be in a different mindset, you are visiting your past life by what you have a mindset.

When you see, what you are seeing from what you have a mindset; you are to change the way you are thinking, you are anchoring by what you have a mindset. You have not to have a good moment, what you have a mindset take your energy and time.

You are victims of your subconscious mind; you are conscious in your conscious mind is the wrong mindset, when you are conscious what you are conscious mind you can not to move forward into what you want to have, you are living the wrong mindset.

What you have a mindset to bring what you have experience in your past life, you are believes, what you have a mindset and to created what you have a feeling. You are not to be comfortable by what you have a feeling what you have a feeling is coming by what you have a mindset.

You are not to be aware; when you change what you have emotional set point. you are unconscious for what you are conscious mindset ; you are still living what you are unconscious mindset, when you are conscious what you are conscious in your conscious mind you can not to change what you have now.

What you have a mindset is your wrong mindset, you are to be keep to go backward for what you want to have; you are congruent the wrong mindset, when you are congruent what you are congruent mindset you are to going past life that what you have experience to be negative.

You are disturb yourself by what you have a mindset; you are to strength what you have emotion, you are to be bored by what you have a day; you are unaware of your mindset and to keep your dram of your life for other day.

You are sticking in your wrong mindset; you can not to be expected to have what you want to have today. You need to be moved a different mindset; when you are moving in a different mindset, you can not to experience what you are experience.

What you have a mindset is your different mindset that you have a mindset is your right mindset; you are not to living in your wrong mindset, if you are living your wrong mindset you can not to change what you have a reality.

To change what you have a reality; you need to live your right mindset, when you live, what you are living mindset; you can not to think, what you are thinking, what you have a mindset is a different mindset that your right mindset.

You are congruent the right mindset; what you are

congruent mindset to bring for you a different experience, you can not to have what you have a wrong feeling you are conscious in your conscious mind is your right mindset. When you are keeping what you are keeping mindset you are to starting to break what you have a mindset and you are to move forward for what you want to have today.

6

YOUR SUBCONSCIOUS MIND FOR WORK

YOU ARE NOT ENJOY WHEN you are doing your work, your subconscious mind is processing a different mindset; you are now living into what you have a mindset, when you live, what you are living mindset to bring a different energy.

You are victims of your subconscious mind; you are not to focus in your work, you are condition of your subconscious mind what you are condition mindset to be conscious in your conscious mind. You are not to do what you want to do for your work you are distracted by what you have a mindset.

You are thinking from what you have a mindset, when you are thinking what your condition of your subconscious mind ; you are to bring a negative energy, what you have a wrong mindset can not to bring for you to have a good moment in your work place.

You are to keep, what you are keeping mindset; you are unconscious of what you have a mindset, when you are unconscious in conscious mind is your wrong mindset, you are to feed your energy into what you have a mindset that what you have a mindset to be distract you what you have a moment.

If you are living most of your time into what you have a mindset you can not to change what you have a reality, what you are condition for your subconscious mind is the wrong mindset, you can not to change what you have a reality, you are to keep, what you have a wrong moment.

To enjoy in your work place; you need to have a right mindset; you are not living in the right mindset you are now living in your wrong mindset. When you are keeping your conscious in your conscious mind is your wrong mindset you can not to change what you have reality.

To have a good moment, it needs to congruent the right mindset; when you are change, what you have a wrong mindset, you are not focusing in your wrong mindset. you are now moving in a different mindset, what you have a mindset is your right mindset ; you can not to have what you have before, you are now living in a different that what you have a mindset is your right mindset you can to have a good energy for your work.

Your subconscious mind not help you, you are not doing your job properly what you have a mindset you are bring when you drive your car that your subconscious mind is processing for congestion; to created a different mindset, what you have a mindset to be a negative mindset, you are now living in your subconscious process mindset and you are bring what you have a mindset in your work place and to live most of time in your wrong mindset

You are victims of your subconscious mind; you are not going forward for your work, you are congruent the wrong mindset. When you are congruent what you are congruent mindset; to give you a low energy, you have not a good feeling, what you have a mindset to created what you have a feeling.

You are disturb by what you have a mindset; you do not to have a good thought, you have a bored moment to have in your work place, what you have a mindset is taking your energy and your time, you are not to control what you have a mindset.

If you are not to control what you have a mindset; you are conscious what you are conscious mind is your wrong mindset, you are to keep what you have a reality what you are conscious in your conscious mind is can not to change what you have a reality.

You are to keep backward for your work; what you have a mindset can to strength what you have a reality. When you are strength what you are strength mindset you are to leak your energy and to have stressed more in your work place.

If you want to do what you want to do in your work place; you need to change what you have a mindset, what you have a mindset can not to give what you want to get in your work place you are congruent the wrong mindset so, you need to be moved on from what you have a mindset.

When you are changing, what you have a mindset; what you have a different mindset is your right mindset, you are not to focusing what you have a mindset before. You are now living in your right mindset; you can not to have what you have realty before.

You are now going forward for your work; you are focusing in your conscious mind is your right mindset, when you are living in your right mind set you can to change what you are feeling before, what you have a mindset to give you what you want to have in your work place.

Your subconscious minds not help you; you are sucking the other person energy, what you have a mindset to have when you heard about something that your subconscious mind is processing a wrong mindset, you are now living in your wrong mindset.

You are victims of your subconscious mind; you are not to do what you want to do in your work, you are distracted by what you have a mindset. When you have what you have a mindset, you can not to get, what you want to get you are congruent the wrong mindset.

What you are congruent mindset to bring a different level energy, you are not to be comfortable by what you have now experience. You are to be bored, what you are conscious in your conscious mind is your wrong mindset, to take your energy.

When you are keeping, what you are keeping the mindset you can to keep backward for what you want to do in your work. To move forward for what you want to do in your work you need to be living in your right mindset, you are now living in the wrong mindset.

So, you need to change, if you want to move forward for what you want to do in your place. When you are changing what you have a mindset you are not to focusing in your wrong mindset, you are to be in a different mindset, what you have a mindset is your right mindset.

When you are living in your right mindset, you can not to activated what you were activating mindset, what you have a mindset is not your wrong mindset, you are now living in your right mindset this your right mindset to be conscious in your conscious mind, you are focusing most of time in your right mindset, you can not to get what you have bored. You are to be living in your right mindset this right mindset to give you what you want to have in your work place

Your subconscious minds not help you ; you are not to move forward for what you want to do in your work place, you are getting what you are getting a mindset, when your workmate comment for your work, your subconscious mind is processing what you have a mindset.

You are living into what you have a mindset, when you are living what you are living mindset you are focusing in your workmate, you are thinking form what you have a mindset is a negative thinking. You are to criticize your friend; you do not to have a good thought for your friend.

You are victims of your subconscious mind; you are to going backward for what you want to do in your work place, you are activating the wrong mindset, when you are activating what you are activating mindset, you can to have the wrong manifestation . what you are congruent mindset is not to bring what you want to have in your work place, you have not to have a vibration match for what you want to have in your work place.

To move forward into what you want to do in your work place ; you need to change what you have a mindset, when you are living what you are living mindset, you can to produce more what you have a wrong mindset that to give you stuck where you are now.

So, you need to change, if you want to move forward into what you want to have in your work place, living in your wrong mindset you can not to be expected to have what you want to have in your work place, you are congruent the wrong mindset.

When you are congruent what you are congruent; you have a mindset that to vibrated differently, you can to attract what you have a wrong realty. So, you need to break what you have a mindset, when you break, what you are breaking mindset you can not to have what you have. You are moving in a different mindset that you are moving mindset is your right mindset; you are now to vibrate what you want to vibrate that to attract what you want to have in your work place.

Your subconscious minds not help you ; you are not to live in your right mindset, what you have a mindset is coming from your subconscious mind process you are bringing your home mindset in your work place, what you have mindset to disconnected you from what you want to do in your work place.

You are not going forward for what you want to have in your work place ; you are now living in your subconscious process mindset, you are to think from what you have a mindset, you are immersed by what you have a mindset you are looking all what you have done in your home.

You are victims of your subconscious mind ; you are not getting from what you have a mindset you are to go backward for what you want to have in your work place, you are to condition into what you have a mindset that to change your physical experience.

When you are thinking what you are thinking, you are congruent in your wrong mindset ; you are to bring a wrong thought that to affected what you are doing, you are giving your energy for the wrong mindset you can to manifested what you have a reality.

If you want to go forward for what you want to have in your work place; you need to know your right mindset you are now living in your wrong mindset, if you are unconscious for what you are conscious in your conscious mind, you are not to change what you have a reality, what you have a realty is anchored by what you have a mindset when you are anchored by what you have a mindset you are to keep what you have experience.

To move forward into what you want to have in your work place; you need to break what you have a mindset, you are still living your wrong mindset you are to stuck where you are, so, you need to be break what you have a mindset, to break what you have a mindset you need to live in a different mindset.

You are now living in a different mindset what you have a mindset is your right mindset; you are not focusing in your wrong mindset you are conscious in your conscious mind is your right mind, you can to start to change what you have a reality, you are focusing in your right mindset you can to start to move toward into what you want to have in your work place.

Your subconscious minds not help you ; you have what you have a feeling is coming from what you have a thought, you are memorizing something that your subconscious mind is processing what you have a mindset, when you are starting to live in your wrong mindset to feel what you are felling.

You are victims of your subconscious mind; you are not going forward into what you want to do in your work place, you are living in your subconscious mind process, when you are living what you are living mindset you can not to change the way you are feeling.

You are congruent the wrong mindset this congruent mindset to be conscious in your conscious mind, you are giving your energy into the wrong mindset that you can not to change what you have a reality, you are anchoring by what you have a mindset.

You are to be keeping to go backward for what you want to do in your workplace; the mindset you have to strength what you have a reality, when you live into what you have a reality to keep what you have experience this you have experience not to give you a good moment in your work place.

To move forward for what you want to have in your work place ; you need to be know what you want to conscious in your work place, you are now to conscious in your conscious mind is the wrong mindset, what you have a wrong mindset can not to change what you have a reality.

To move forward into what you want to have ; you need to congruent the right mindset, when you are congruent what you are congruent mindset you can to go backward for what you want to have in your work place you are congruent the wrong mindset in your conscious mind.

So, you need to be moving into your right mindset, if you want to have what you want to have in your work place you are now living in your wrong mindset you can not to change what you have a reality what you have a mindset can to give what you have you reality that not to give you what you want to have in your work place but, moving into you right mindset and to conscious in your conscious mindset is your right mindset, you are to starting to change what you have a reality you are to go forward for what you want to have in your work place, what you have a mindset is your right mindset that you have a mindset to magnetized what you want to have in your work place.

Your subconscious minds not help you; you are condition of your daily ritual of mindset, your subconscious mind is processing for you to have what you have a mindset, you are not to be enjoying in your work place you are distracted by what you have a mindset; when you are living into what you have a mindset you can to created a resisting for your work, you are stressed out by what you have a mindset.

You are victims of your subconscious mind ; you are not to go forward for what you want to have in your work place, you are living in the wrong mindset when you are living what you are living mindset, you can to keep to go backward for what you want to have in your work place.

You are unaware of your mindset, what you have a mindset to created for you a distraction for what you want to have a work place and your healthy; when you are conscious what you are conscious mindset most of time in your conscious mind, you can to have unpleasant moment in your work place you are congruent the wrong mindset you can not to be expected form what you have a mindset to have a pleasant moment and to have what you want to have in your work place.

To move forward for what you want to have in your work place; you need to be change what you have a mindset if you are living what you are living mindset you can to keep what you have a reality what you have a mindset is not to bring for you to have what you want to have in your work place.

You are living in the wrong mindset; the wrong mindset always to give what you do not want to have, you are not congruent of vibration match, what you have a vibration is coming from what you have a mindset when you are vibrate what you are vibrating you can to attracting what you are attracting that what you do not want to have in your work place.

To get what you want to get in your work place; you need to know you right mindset not knowing your right mindset you can to keep what you are keeping mindset this you wrong mindset have not to have a vibration match for what you want to have in your work place, to get the vibration match you need to change the mindset.

But, living what you have a wrong mindset you can to keep backward for what you want to have in your work place, to move forward for what you want to have you need to break what you have a mindset when you are breaking what you are breaking mindset and to conscious in your conscious mind is a different mindset what you have a mindset is your right mindset, you are to starting to change what you have a vibration what you have a vibration to match into what you want to have in your work place, you are to moving forward into what you want to have in your work place.

Your subconscious minds not help you ; you are doing what you are doing by what you have a mindset, you are living in a different mindset you are not knowing your right mindset your subconscious mind is processing a different mindset, you are to live into what you have a mindset.

You are to be a victim of your subconscious mind; what you have a mindset not to strength of what you want to have in your work place, you are not living in your right mindset you are now living in your subconscious mind process mindset that you have a wrong mindset to strength what you have now reality.

You are not going forward for what you want to have in your workplace; you are conscious in your conscious mind is your wrong mindset, you are to manifested what you do not want that to bring for you to go backward into what you want to have in your work place.

If you live consciously and subconsciously into what you have a mindset; you are to get more of what you do not want to have in your work place, what you have a mindset to strength not to have what you want to have, you are not to be expected from what you have a mindset to have what you want to have.

You are congruent the wrong mindset ; when you are congruent what you are congruent mindset you can to activated what you are activating that you have a reality, to distracted what you have a moment in your work place.

To get what you want to get in your work place; you need to be living in the right mindset, you are not living in the right mindset what you have a mindset is your subconscious mind process that your subconscious mind to give you what you have a negative mindset, you are conscious most time in your conscious mind is the wrong mindset, you can not to move forward from what you have a mindset you are to resisting into what you want to have in your work place.

To move forward into what you want to have in your work place ; you need to change what you have a mindset when you are changing what you are changing mindset, you can not to have what you have a reality, when you are changing into a different mindset that you have a mindset is your right mindset, you are now focusing in your conscious mindset is your right mindset most of time you can to start to change what you have a reality, what you have a mindset is your right mindset that to bring for you to have what you want to have in your work place.

Your subconscious minds not help you; you are condition into your subconscious mindset, when you are condition what you are condition from your subconscious mind that you have a mindset is the wrong mindset, you are now staying into what you have a mindset.

You are not too aware your right mindset; you can not to move forward for what you want to have in your work place, what you have a mindset is bring the wrong attitude into what you want to do in your work place, you are giving your focus into your wrong mindset, when you are focusing what you are focusing mindset, you can not to change what you have attitude

You are victims of your subconscious of mind; you are congruent the wrong mindset what you are congruent mindset to change what you have attitude, you have not a time to have your right mindset you are easily condition into your subconscious mind process, you are to conscious most of time in your conscious mind is your wrong mindset.

You are to keep to go backward into what you want to have in your work place; what you have a mindset can not to change what you have a reality, what you have a mindset to strength what you have a reality, you are too distracted by what you have a mindset you are not living in the right mindset, when you have what you have a mindset, you are to wasted your energy and time.

To move forward into what you want to have in your workplace; you need to be to know you right mindset, you are unconscious for your right mindset, you can not to have what you want to have in your work place, when you are living most of time into unconscious mindset you are to be victims of your subconscious mind.

To move forward into what you want to have in your work place; you need to be to know your right mindset, when you do not know your right mindset you can not to change what you have a reality what you have reality is coming from what you have a mindset that to bring not to move forward into what you want to have in your workplace.

To have what you want to have in your workplace; you need to break what you have a mindset, if you are not to break what you have a mindset, you are to focus in your conscious mind is your wrong mindset you can to strength what you have a reality, you can not to change from what you have a mindset what you have a reality, to change what you have a realty you need to break what you have a mindset, when you are breaking what you are breaking mindset, you are focusing in your conscious mind is your right mindset, you are living most of time your right mindset you are to move into what you want to have in your work place what you have a mindset to magnetized what you want to have.

7

YOUR SUBCONSCIOUS MIND FOR YOUR ENVIRONMENT

YOUR SUBCONSCIOUS MINDS NOT HELP you; you can not to have a good mindset for your environment, your subconscious mind is processing when you are in a café that you have a mindset not to give you a pleasure moment, when you have a moment in the café.

What you have a plan, to be enjoy in the café but, your subconscious mind is processing what you have a mindset, you are conscious what you are conscious mind is your wrong mindset; when you are conscious what you are conscious in your conscious mind is your wrong mindset you can not to have a happy moment in the café, by what you have a mindset.

You are victims of your subconscious mind; the mindset you have, to distract your moment, you are not to live in the right mindset; you are now living in the wrong mindset when you are thinking from what you have a mindset you can not to get positive energy.

What you have a mindset to take your energy and time, when you are keeping what you are keeping mindset you are to be blind for what you have a mindset; when you are blind into what you have a mindset you are to keep the tragedy of your blind mindset.

You are focusing in your conscious mindset is the wrong mindset; you do not to get a good time in the café, you are feeding your energy into the wrong mindset what you are feeding mindset can to created for you what you have a reality in the café.

To get what you want to get; you need to be living the right mindset, you are not to live in the right mindset what you have a mindset is the wrong mindset; you cannot expected to change what you have a reality from what you have a mindset.

You need to break what you have a mindset ; when are breaking what you are breaking mindset, you can not to have what you have a realty, moving into a different mindset that you have a mindset is the right mindset you can to break what you have a reality, what you have a mindset is your right mindset you are now to conscious in your conscious mind is your right mindset in the café, you are to break what you have emotional realty and to have what you want to have in the café, what you have a mindset to have a different vibration that to attract a pleasure moment in the café.

Your subconscious minds not help you; when you are walking you do not to have what you want to have a mindset your subconscious mind is condition into outside place that you are condition of mindset to have in your conscious mindset.

You are not to be present; you are distracted by what you have a mindset, when you are living what you are living mindset, to be angry you are not to created a good time you are living in the wrong mindset what you are conscious in your conscious mind is your wrong mindset that to bring a different feeling, you are engaging into the wrong mindset, you are disturbs yourself when you are engaging what you are engaging mindset.

You are victims of your subconscious mind; you can not to have what you want to have from what you have a mindset, you are congruent the wrong mindset when you are congruent what you are congruent mindset you can to active what you are activating mindset that to bring more what you have now.

To have a good walking; you have to living in the right mindset, you are not living in the right mindset now, you are condition into your subconscious mind process what you are condition mindset is in your conscious mind; you are focusing in your wrong mindset, you are toasted by what you have a thought you can not to have what you want to have from what you have a mindset.

To get forward for what you want to have; you have to living into the right mindset, to live into your right mindset you need to be change what you have a mindset, when you are changing what you are changing mindset you can to have what you have a thought and feeling what you have a mindset can to give you what you do not want to have.

So, you need to break it ; when you are breaking what you are breaking mindset, you are to live into the right mindset you are not to conscious what you are conscious in you are conscious mind, you are focusing in your conscious mind is your right mindset, you can not to activating what you were activating reality, you are now living in a different mindset that you have a mindset is your right mindset, you are to get what you want to get; when you are walking, you are starting to enjoy by what you have a moment.

Your subconscious minds not help you; you are sitting down in the river but what you have a mindset not to give you a pleasure time you are condition of your subconscious mind, what you are condition of your subconscious mind is the wrong mindset, you are now focusing into what you have a mindset you are not to control of what you have a mindset.

You are victims of your subconscious mind; you are affected by what you have a mindset, you can not to be present, you can not to be enjoy and you are to be distract by what you have a mindset. You are aligned the wrong mindset what you are aligned mindset to rub your time.

You want to have what you want to have ; need to know your right mindset, you are not living in your right mindset when you are sitting down in the river you are condition into your subconscious mind, what you are condition of your subconscious mind is the wrong mindset.

You are now most of time you are living in the wrong mindset; when you are living what you are living mindset in your conscious mind is your wrong mindset, you can not to change what you have a reality what you have a mindset can to give you what you have now.

You are going into the river; you want to enjoy when you see the view but, you are not seeing what you are want seeing; having a different view from what you have a mindset and to see what you have now, what you have now not to give you enjoy.

You are aligned in the wrong mindset when you are sitting down in the river, what you are aligned mindsets, do not to have a happy moment you are living in the wrong mindset, to go forward into what you want to have in the river, you need to be knowing your right mindset.

So, to move forward for what you want to have in the river; you have to break what you have a mindset, focusing what you are focusing mindset can not to change what you have a moment in the river, you are too stuck into what you have a bored moment.

But, breaking what you have a mindset; you can not to have what you have a reality, when you are moving into a different mindset what you have a mindset is the right mindset you can to break the reality, you are not living in the wrong mindset you are now living a different mindset what you have a mindset to be is the right mindset, you are now focusing in your conscious mind is your right mindset you are to gravitated what you want to have in the river.

Your subconscious minds not help you; you are not living in the right mindset when you have a time with your friend you are condition of your friend mindset you are to be living in the wrong mindset, your subconscious mind is processing the wrong mindset that it looks like your friend mindset, you are now living in the wrong mindset you can to change what you have emotional set point.

You are victims of your subconscious mind; you can not to get fun with your friend, you are condition into your wrong mindset what you are condition mindset to be the wrong mindset, when you are living the wrong mindset you can to be living in bored mindset.

What you are conscious in your conscious mind is the wrong mindset; you can not to get a happy moment with your friend, what you are conscious in your conscious mind not to give what you want to have a time with friend, you are unaware of the right mindset when you are unaware of the right mindset you can to keep what you have emotional set point.

You are too suffered by what you have a mindset ; what you have a mindset can to give not to be happy with your moment, what you have a mindset to give a resisting not to have what you want to have a time with your friend.

To get what you want to get a good time with friend ; you need to be know the right mindset, you are not living in the right mindset what you have a mindset is the wrong mindset you are living most of time into your wrong mindset you can not to change from what you have a mindset.

To have what you want to have a time with friend; you need to be break what you have a mindset, to break what you have a mindset you have to live in a different mindset, when you are living in a different mindset you cannot to get what you have now but, when you are moving in a different mindset you have to know the right mindset, not knowing your right mindset to cost your energy and time.

You are now living in your right mindset ; you can not to have what you had before, when you are moving into your right mindset you are conscious in your conscious mind is your right mindset what you have a mindset can to give you what you want to have a time with your friend.

Your subconscious minds not help you; you are condition

for someone when you see him, your subconscious mind is processing for what you are condition that you have a mindset to be the wrong mindset, you are not to enjoying by what you have a time what you have a mindset is distracted your moment.

You are victims of your subconscious mind; you want to enjoy when you are in the park but you are condition into your subconscious mind, you are now conscious in your conscious mind is the wrong mindset what you have a mindset is not to bring a good moment in the park.

You are congruent the wrong mindset when you are congruent what you are congruent mindset, you can to strength what you have a realty this you have a realty can not to give you what you want to have, you are aligned the wrong mindset.

If you are conscious what you are conscious in your conscious mind is your wrong mindset, you are sticking in the wrong mindset, you are incompetence to conscious your right mindset in conscious mind, your competence is living the wrong mind set in your conscious mind, and you are to go backward for what you want to have.

To get what you want to get; you need to be moved from what you have a mindset, you are aligned the wrong mindset what you have a mindset can not to change the way you see the moment, what you have a mindset to keep, to feed you what you have now.

To move forward into what you want to have ; need to break what you have a mindset, to break what you have a mindset you need to change your focus, you are now focusing in the wrong mindset that you are focusing mindset to gravitated more what you have now but, moving into your right mindset to break what you have a realty, when you are focusing into your right mindset you are to starting to change what you have a realty what you have a mindset to bring what you want to have.

Your subconscious minds not help you; you are disturbing by what you have a mindset, when you are sitting in your invitation place you are hearing someone blame you, your subconscious mind is processing the wrong mindset you are now living in the wrong mindset, you are losing your peace life what you have a mindset is disturbing yourself.

You are victims of your subconscious mind; you are slipping over the wrong mindset, you are unable to have the right mindset you are conscious in your conscious mind is the wrong mindset; when you are conscious what you are conscious mind you can to active what you are activating mindset this the wrong mindset to give more to stressful in your time.

You are not to have what you want to have, you are aligning the wrong mindset when you are aligning the wrong mindset what you have a mindset to distract a peaceful life, you are not to think a good thought from what you have a mindset what you have a thought to toast you.

You are going backward for what you want to have ; you are most of time conscious in your conscious mind is your wrong mindset, you can not to change from what you have a mindset your energy level what you have a mindset is the wrong mindset to created for to have what you do not want to have.

To be happy in your invitation ; you need to be living in the right mindset, you are now condition into the wrong mindset when you are condition what you are condition mindset you are to keep gravitated what you have now that to give more stressful moment in your invitation.

So, you need to be living in the right mindset ; if you want to get what you want to get when you are moving in a different mindset you are not to strength what you have a realty what you have a mindset is a different mindset that you have a mindset to be your right mindset, you can to starting break what you have a realty because you are now living in your right mindset this your right mindset to have a different vibration than what you have a vibration, what you have a vibration is the right vibration that to attract what you want to have a moment.

Your subconscious minds not help you; when you are in the shop you have angry mindset, your subconscious mind is processing when you see old friend, you are now to have a different mindset you are now focusing in your conscious mind is the wrong mindset, what you have a mindset to bring a different behavior you are not to be happy by what you are feeling what you have a mindset to distract you, you do not to have a good moment in your shopping.

You are victims of your subconscious mind; when you see the old friend your subconscious mindset is processing the wrong mindset you are now living in your shop a different mindset this you have a mindset to create the wrong thought and feeling.

You are not to be present when you are in shop ; you are cutting by what you have a mindset you are focusing in your conscious mind set is the wrong mindset, you are to be angry what you have a mindset to create for you to be angry in your shop, you are not control what you have a mindset, the mindset you have to control you, you are unconscious for what you are conscious you are to be keeping staying in your conscious mind is your wrong mindset.

When you are keeping what you are keeping mindset you can not to change what you have a behavior, what you have a behavior is coming from what you have a mindset when you are focusing what you are focusing mindset you are to feed your energy into your wrong mindset that to keep what you have a behavior.

You can not to enjoy in your shop; what you have a mindset to bring you to go backward for what you want to have in the shop, to get what you want to get in your shop you need to know the right mindset, if you do not know your right mindset.

You are easily to condition of your subconscious mind process, you can to bring a different mindset when you are living in the wrong mindset what you have a mindset can to give you what you have a realty, you can not to be expected to change form what you have a mindset to have what you want to have, if you want to have what you want to have you need to break what you have a mindset when you are breaking what you have a mindset you can to change what you have a behavior what you have a mindset is your right mindset that to give you what you want to have in your shop.

Your subconscious minds not help you ; you are not to living in the right mindset when you are in spa your subconscious minds is processing the habitual mindset ; you are now to be busy by what you have a mindset, you are going to have enjoyment in the spa but you have a different mindset.

You are victims of your subconscious mind; when you have what you have a mindset, you are to going in a different energy level what you have a mindset not to give you a good energy level you are living in the wrong mindset when you are living what you are living mindset you are to leak your energy you are aligned the wrong mindset.

You are not to have what you want to have in the spa; what you are aligned mindset to give you upset when you are in the spa because what you have a mindset to gravitated what you are thinking from what you have a mindset cannot to be expected a good thing, you are living the wrong mindset you are focusing in your conscious mind is your wrong mindset.

When you are conscious in your conscious mind is your wrong mindset; you are to strength what you have a reality this you have realty can not to give you what you want to have in the spa, you are conscious the wrong mindset when you conscious what you are conscious mindset, you can not to change the way you are thinking and feeling you are anchoring yourself in the wrong mindset.

To move forward for what you want to have in the spa; you need to live the right mindset, you are not living in the right mindset you are unconscious for your right mindset when you are unconscious for your right mindset ; you are conscious in your conscious mind is you wrong mindset.

You can not to go forward for what you want to have in the sap; to get what you want to get in the spa, you need to be to know what to conscious, not knowing your right mindset and to conscious what you are conscious in your conscious mind to keep what you have a realty that you do not want to have a realty.

So, you need to be moving in a different mindset, if you want to have what you want to have in the spa. When you are moving in a different mindset what you have a mindset is your right mindset you are not to bringing what you have a reality, you are living in a different mindset this the different mindset can to bring a different realty, what you have a realty to give you what you want to have in the spa.

Your subconscious minds not help you ; you are now living what you have a mindset your subconscious mind is processing a different mindset you can not to staying in the right mindset you are to condition into your subconscious mind you can not to have a good moment in the library, you are now living in the wrong mindset what you have a mindset to take your focus, when you are focusing what you are focusing in the conscious mind is what you have a mindset you are to start disconnected from your right mindset.

You are victims of your subconscious mind; what you are aligning mindset can not to give you, what you want to have in the library. When you are shift; you are focusing in your subconscious mind process you can to have a wrong attitude toward into what you want to do, you are unconsciously to change your energy level what you have a mindset have a different vibration you are now living most of your time in your wrong mindset.

You can to go backward for what you want to have; you are controlling by what you have a mindset, when you are controlling by what you have a mindset you are to strength what you have a realty that you do not want to have, if you are keeping what you are keeping mindset you are to immersed yourself in the wrong mindset that to feed you more to have what you have now.

To move forward into what you want to have; you need to break what you have a mindset, you are now living most of time in the wrong mindset when you live most of time in the wrong mindset you are to strength more what you have a mindset, to break what you have a mindset you need to know your right mindset not knowing your right mindset to wasted your time in the library.

To get what you want to get; it needs the right mindset, you are still living in the wrong mindset when you are still aligned what you are aligned mindset you can not to change what you have a reality, you are still condition into what you have a mindset what you have a mindset can not to change what you have a reality.

To move forward into what you want to have in the library ; you need to be aligned the right mindset not what you are aligned mindset what you are aligned the wrong mindset, you need to be living in the different mindset when you are moving into a different mindset what you have a mindset is your right mindset.

You are conscious in your conscious mind is your right mindset; you are not living in the wrong mindset, you are conscious most of time in your conscious mind is your right mindset you can not to create what you were creating reality you are aligned the right mindset that what you have a mindset to give you in the library what you want to have.

8

YOUR SUBCONSCIOUS
MIND FOR YOUR TIME

YOUR SUBCONSCIOUS MINDS NOT HELP you, you are not living in your right mindset, you are now living in your subconscious mind process ; you are not focusing in your desire you are distracted by your subconscious mind, when you live in the wrong mindset you are to wasted your time.

You are victims of your subconscious mind ; you are not to consumed your time, when you are living in the wrong mindset you can not to finished what you want to finish what you have a mindset to distract you, you are living in the wrong mindset what you are aligned mindset to take your time.

You are not to go forward for what you want to finished ; you are conscious in your conscious mind is the wrong mind, when you are conscious what you are conscious mind you are fully to give the wrong mindset this the mindset you have, to give you to go backward for what you want to finished.

When you are living most of time in the wrong mindset ; you are control by what you have a mindset, this mindset is not to bringing what you want to finished instead to keep what you have now, to get what you want to get you need to have a time and the right mindset.

You are wasting most of time by what you have a mindset this you have a mindset is coming from subconscious process, you can not to change a realty from what you have a mindset you are conscious in the wrong mindset, you are unconscious for what you have a mindset when you are wasted your time when you are unconscious for what you have a mindset, you are competence in your conscious mind is the wrong mindset that you are to conscious in your conscious mind is the wrong mindset, you are to go forward for what you have a wrong mindset that not to bring what you want to finished.

To move forward into what you want to finished ; you need to be to know your right mindset, unconscious your right mindset and conscious in your conscious mind is the wrong mindset you can not to get what you want to get from what you have a mindset.

You need to be living in the right mindset; when you are breaking what you have a wrong mindset, you are moving in a different mindset this you have a mindset is the right mindset you can not to go backward for what you want to finished you are focusing in conscious mind is the right mindset you are to consumed your time and to get what you want to get.

Your subconscious minds not help you; you are distracted

by your subconscious mind you are not to enjoy your time by what you have a mindset this the mindset you have, when you see what you are seeing to bring what you have a mindset, your subconscious mind is processing the wrong mindset you are now starting to live in the wrong mindset.

You are victims of your subconscious mind; you can not to consumed your time, you are living in the wrong mindset what you have a mindset to waste your time and your energy. You are conscious in your conscious mind is the wrong mindset you can not to enjoy your time by what you have a mindset.

What you have a time take by what you have a mindset; the mindset you have cannot to give you, to have what you want to have, you are aligned the wrong mindset this you have a mindset is coming from your subconscious mind process.

You are now most of time to live in the wrong mindset; you cannot to go forward for what you want to have a time, what you have a time to be distracted by what you have a mindset, you do not to have a good way looking from what you have a mindset you are congruent the wrong mindset.

When you are living what you are living mindset you are to waste your time, you can not to be expected from what you have a mindset to have what you want to have enjoy, you are focusing the wrong mindset.

What you are focusing in your conscious mind is your wrong mindset this the mindset you have to active what you are activating, you are not to be expected with your time to have what you want to have enjoyment, the time you have to be congruent the wrong mindset.

To get what you want to get with your time ; you have to know what you are focusing, you are focusing in your conscious mind is the wrong mindset you are to be bored with your time, you can not to get a good energy from what you have a mindset.

You need to be know your right mindset; when you know your right mindset you can not to wasted your time but you are to be unconscious for your right mindset and to conscious the wrong mindset, you can to magnetized what you are magnetized that to be a bored moment.

So, you need to break what you have a mindset if you want to use your time, living what you are living mindset can not to change your energy level but knowing your right mindset and to change what you are focusing in your conscious mind, you are now focusing in your conscious mind is your right mindset you cannot wasted your time you are conscious the right mindset, you can to have what you want to have enjoyment.

Your subconscious minds not to helps you; you are not to live in your right mindset, what you have a mindset to have from your subconscious mind, your subconscious mind is processing to memorizing something, you are now conscious in your conscious mind is what you have a mindset, you want to use your time for doing something but you are distracted by what you have a mindset.

You are victims of your subconscious mind ; you are not staying into what you want to do with your time, you are now living in the wrong mindset when you are living what you have a mindset you are to strength the wrong mindset you are to be wasted your time.

What you have a mindset is coming from your

subconscious mind process, you are to aligned what you have a mindset with your time, you can not to do what you want to do in your time, what you have a mindset with your time to give not to have what you want to have with your time.

You are not going forward for what you want to do with your time ; you are control by what you have a mindset this you have a mindset is coming from your subconscious mind, you are now living most of time to be not the right mindset you are to living in the wrong mindset.

You are too conscious most of time in your conscious mind is your wrong mindset; when you are living most of time in the wrong mindset you cannot to change what you have a realty. What you have a mindset is coming from your subconscious mind, you are conscious what you are conscious is the wrong mindset you can to keep to strength what you have a reality you are wasting your time by what you have the wrong mindset.

To get what you want to get with your time; you need to be aligned the right mindset, you are now aligned with your time the wrong mindset, what you have a mindset to take your time and your energy you are to keep to go backward for what you want to do with your time.

To move forward for what you want to do with your time ; you need to be break what you have a mindset when you are breaking what you are breaking mindset you can not to strength what you have a realty with your time.

Moving into a different mindset with your time you are to moving into the right mindset when you are moving into your right mindset you cannot to strength what you have a realty, you are now living in a different mindset this you have a mindset is your right mindset you can to break what you have a reality, what you have a mindset with your time is the right mindset, you are now living in the right mindset you can to magnetized what you want to magnetized with your time.

Your subconscious minds not help you ; you are not to live in the right mindset you are distracted by your environment you are seeing your old girlfriend your subconscious mind is processing the wrong mindset what you have a mindset is the wrong mindset with your time you are not to be fun by what you have a mindset you are to change your energy level, you are conscious in your conscious mind is your subconscious mind process mindset, you are unable to have a fun with your time you are totally distracted by what you have a mindset.

You are victims of your subconscious mind; you are not living with your time in the right mindset what you have a mindset to give you with your time to have an upset moment, you are focusing most of time in your conscious mind is your wrong mindset.

What you have a mindset is your wrong mindset to take your time; you cannot to go forward for what you want to do with your time, you are now aligned the wrong mindset this you have a mindset to bring with your time to be upset.

You can not to change what you have a reality by what you have a mindset instead what you have a mindset to give more what you have a realty that to distract your time and your energy, by what you have a mindset just to keep what you have now, you are most of time living in the wrong mindset you are not to consumed your time by what you have a mindset this you have a mindset to wasted your time.

To have a fun with your time; you need to be aware your right mindset, you are now to condition your wrong mindset when you are condition what you have a mindset what you have a mindset is your wrong mindset that what you have a mindset to give, to be upset in your moment.

You are victims of your subconscious mind; you are living what you are living most of time is your wrong mindset when you are living what you are living most of time that you have is the wrong mindset you can to keep what you have energy and to wasted your time.

So, you need to be moving in your right mindset if you want to have a fun with your time ; you are to breaking what you have a mindset you are now focusing in a different mindset you are not to focus in your wrong mindset, you are to change your focus what you are focusing mindset is your right mindset you can not to have a upset moment by what you have a mindset you are living is a different mindset what you have a mindset to bring for you to have a fun with your time.

Your subconscious minds not help you; you are to be living in the wrong mindset, your subconscious mind is processing a different mindset what you have a mindset to distract what you do with your time, you are unable to concentrated in your right mindset, you are now living in the wrong mindset.

You are victims of your subconscious mind; you are not to concentrated with your time what you wanted, you are now living in your wrong mindset that you are bring from your subconscious mind, you are to concentrated in your conscious mind is your wrong mindset.

When you are concentrating what you are concentrate is the wrong mindset ; you are to feed your energy in the wrong mindset, you are to wasted your time in the wrong mindset what you have a mindset is bring for you to have a distraction that not to do what you want to do with your time.

When you are keeping what you are keeping concentration mindset you cannot to change what you have a reality, what you have a mindset is to give you what you have a reality with your time, you are conscious most of time in your conscious mind is the wrong mindset.

You can not to go forward for what you want to do with your time; you are congruent the wrong mindset when you are congruent what you are congruent mindset you can not to change what you have a reality with your time, you are aligned with your time the wrong mindset.

To get what you want to get with your time; you need to be change the mindset you have now, you are now most of time living in the wrong mindset when you are living what you are living mindset you are to be anchoring your energy by what you have a mindset, you are wasted your time and your energy.

To move forward for what you want to do; you need to use your time properly, you are not living in your right mindset if you are not living in your right mindset you are wasted your time for wrong mindset what you have a mindset can not to give what you want to have instead to give you to go backward for what you want to do.

But, living in a different mindset this you have a mindset

is your right mindset, you can not to wasted your energy and your time, you are concentrating in your conscious mind is your right, when you are concentrating what you are concentrate you can not to have what you had reality you are now living is a different mindset that you have a mindset is your right mindset, you can to break what you have a reality by what you have a mindset and to have what you want to have with your time.

Your subconscious minds not help you ; you are not to success for what you want to do, you are living in your subconscious mindset when you are doing what you are doing your subconscious mind is processing, to be doubt in your what you want to do with your time.

What you have a mindset, to be with your time, to have what you have the mindset this you have a mindset is your wrong mindset, you can not to get what you want to get success you are conscious in your conscious mind is your wrong mindset this you have a mindset to distracted what you want to do.

You are victims of your subconscious mind; you are to living in the wrong mindset when you are living what you have a mindset you can to get what you have a realty this you have a realty can not to give you to have what you want to have success, you are strength the wrong mindset, what you have a mindset is the wrong mindset to created a different realty that to go backward for what you want to have success.

You are aligned the wrong mindset when you are aligned what you are aligned mindset you are using the time for what you are aligned mindset this you aligned mindset is the wrong mindset you can to created more to have what you have now reality.

When you are most of time to live in your wrong mindset, you are not to control what you have a mindset instead the mindset you have is controlled your conscious mind, you are conscious in your conscious mind is your wrong mindset, you are giving your energy for your wrong mindset you are to be keeping to strength what you have a realty.

To get what you want do ; you need to be aware your mindset, you are not aware your mindset you are now living most of time is in the wrong mindset what you have a mindset to take your time and to distract what you want to do.

When you are distracted by what you have a mindset; you are wasting your time in the wrong mindset you are not conscious in your conscious mind is your right mindset, you are focusing in your conscious mind is the wrong mindset with your time.

To move forward for what you want to have success; you need to be breaking what you have a mindset when you are breaking what you have a mindset and to move a different mindset this you have a mindset is your right mindset, you are focusing in your conscious mind is your right mindset, you are not focusing the wrong mindset in your conscious mind, you are to break what you have a reality you are now living in your right mindset with your time, what you have a mindset to created a different realty that what you want to have a success.

9

YOUR SUBCONSCIOUS MIND FOR YOUR DESIER

YOUR SUBCONSCIOUS MINDS NOT HELP you ; you have a desire to focus for what you want to do today but you are subconsciously to conscious in your conscious mind is your subconscious mind process, what you are conscious in your conscious mind is to change what you have energy level.

You are unable to be focusing in your desire; when you are change what you are change mindset you are to congruent the wrong mindset when you are congruent what you have a mindset what you have a mindset to take your focus in your conscious mind, when you are conscious what you are conscious mindset is the wrong mindset you can to manifested the wrong realty.

You are victims of your subconscious mind; you are living not your right mindset what you have a mindset is the wrong mindset, to give you, to go backward for your desire; you can not to get your desire by what you have a mindset.

You are focusing in your conscious mind is your subconscious mind process ; what you are focusing mindset to take your time and energy, when you are take your energy by what you have a mindset, you are now to be sluggish and you are to resist in your desire, what you have a mindset to anchoring your energy level.

You are not to move forward for your desire; to get your desire you need to be living in your right mindset, you are not living in your right mindset what you are conscious most of your time in your conscious mind is the wrong mindset.

When you are living in the wrong mindset you can not to change what you have energy level, what you have energy level is coming from by what you have a mindset, you are to distract your desire and you are too distracted your healthy by what you have a mindset, what you have a mindset to bring a low level energy.

To move forward for your desire; you need to be moving into a different mindset, living into what you have a mindset to give you, to have backward for your desire and to be sluggish. So, you need to be living in the right mindset.

To live in your right mindset you have to be breaking what you have a mindset ; aligned what you are aligned the wrong mindset is creating what you have a realty so, you need to be aligned the right mindset , to aligned your right mindset you need to be change what you are focusing in your conscious mind, when you are focusing in your conscious mind is your right mindset you are to breaking what you are aligning the wrong mindset, you are now focusing in your conscious mind is your right mindset you are to attract what you want to have a desire.

Your subconscious minds not help you; you have a desire to have a good time with your friends but your subconscious mind processing is the same mindset with your friend, you are to pick is your friend aura when you have what you have an aura, you do not to have what you have a feeling.

You are victims of your subconscious mind; you are not living into the right mindset, when you are meeting with your friend, you have a desire to have a good time with your friend but your friend have not to have a good mindset, you are picking what your friend have a feeling.

You are unconscious for the right mindset you are just to pick your friend mindset ; when you are living into what you have a mindset you can not to get what you want to get a good time, you are now focusing in your conscious mind is the wrong mindset.

What you have a mindset is not, bring what you want to have a good time you are aligned your friend mindset when you are aligned what you are aligned mindset you can to get what you have now, this you have now is, to disturb what you want to have a good time.

Living most of time into what you have a mindset ; to activating what you are activating energy this you have energy is coming from what you have a mindset when you are most of time to conscious in your conscious mind is what you have a mindset.

You are to be anchoring in the wrong mindset ; when you anchor by what you have a mindset, you are not to change the way you are feeling you are too distracted your time by what you have a mindset you are, to move backward for what you want to have a good day.

To have what you want to have a good time; you need to be aware your mindset, you are now living in the wrong mindset when you are living in the wrong mindset you can not to change what you have a reality what you have a mindset is giving you to feel what you are feeling that to be not get a good time in your moment.

But, moving in a different mindset, you are moving in your right mindset you can not to get what you have now, what you have a mindset is your right mindset when you are living in your right mindset you can to start to change what you were feeling, you are in a different mindset what you have a mindset is your right mindset you are now conscious in your conscious mind is your right mindset you are to feel differently than what you were feeling, you are to going into your desire that what you want to have a good time with your friend.

Your subconscious minds not help you; you have what you have a mindset when you see someone you have a desire for yourself to have happy moment but you are going into your subconscious mind, you have a mindset is coming from your subconscious mind process, you are now, not to living in your right mindset you are distracted by what you are condition mindset that your subconscious mind process for what you have seen.

You are victims of your subconscious mind ; you cannot to have what you want to have a desire for yourself, your psychic force take by what you have a wrong mindset, when you are conscious what you are conscious in your conscious mind is wrong mindset.

You can not to have a happy moment, you are aligned the wrong mindset what you have a mindset can to give, to have a distraction for what you want to have a desire, when you are focusing in your conscious mind is your wrong mindset you can to go backward for what you want to have.

You are focusing in your conscious mind is the wrong mindset ; you are thinking from what you have a mindset you can not to have a good thought from what you have a mindset instead you are to be toasted by what you have a thought.

You are a desire to have a happy moment for yourself ; you are condition into your subconscious mind when you are condition what you have a mindset you are to change your energy level what you are aligned mindset is bring for you to have what you do not to have a moment.

You are controlling by what you have a mindset in your conscious mindset, when you are conscious what you are conscious mindset in your conscious mindset you can to strength what you have a realty that you have a realty is giving you not to have your desire.

You are going backward for your desire; you are most of time is living in the wrong mindset, when you are living what you are living mindset you can not to change what you have a realty what you have a mindset is the wrong mindset to give, to have what you have a though and feeling.

To get what you want to have a desire for yourself ; you need to be moving into your right mindset, you are not living in your right mindset what you have a mindset is your wrong mindset so, you need a different mindset when you are moving in a different mindset what you have a mindset is your right mindset you can not to magnetized what you were magnetized, you are change your focus when you change your focus, your psychic force to be in your right mindset you are to have what you want to have a happy moment for yourself.

Your subconscious minds not to help you ; you have a desire to read a book but you are not to be into your right mindset your subconscious mind is processing and to give you what you have a mindset you are now living in your wrong mindset.

You are victims of your subconscious mind ; what you have a mindset is the wrong mindset you are to be resisting into what you want to do when you are conscious what you are conscious in your conscious mind is the wrong mindset you can not to do what you want to do.

You are giving your focus for your wrong mindset, when you are staying in your wrong mindset you can be stressful, you do not to have a good energy you have a low self – esteem for what you want to do, you are to go backward for your desire.

You are conscious in your conscious mind is the wrong mindset, what you have a mindset is strength your stress, you are to be easily to be sick you are to give your energy for your wrong mindset, what you have a mindset is bring for you to have what you have a stressful moment and to be to go backward for your desire.

You can not to get what you want to get by what you have a mindset ; you do not to have a vibration match for your desire, you are conscious what you are conscious in your conscious mind is your wrong mindset this you have a mindset to have a different vibration.

When you are vibrating what you are vibrating, what you have a vibration is a different vibration when you are holding what you are holding vibration you can to keep to attract what you are attracting to be a stressful life and to be stuck in what you have a mindset.

To get what you want to get ; you have to be aware your right mindset, if you are unconscious for your right mindset you can not to get your desire, you are now most of time to conscious in your conscious mind is your wrong mindset.

When you are congruent what you are congruent mindset, you can not to change what you have a realty what you have a mindset to give you the wrong vibration when you are living in your wrong vibration you can to attract what you do not want.

So, you need to be living in the right mindset if you want to have what you want a desire, when you are moving in a different mindset you can to be breaking what you have a mindset, you are now focusing in your right mindset what you have a mindset to give a match of vibration, you are to go forward for your desire and to have what you want to have.

Your subconscious minds not help you; you are not living in good mindset, you have a desire to have a good time with your wife but your subconscious mind is distracted what you have a mindset you are now to live in the wrong mindset, what you have a jealous mindset is to bring not to have a good moment, your subconscious mind is processing when your wife has a conversation with phone.

You are victims of your subconscious mind; you are not to go forward for your desire you are living in the wrong mindset what you have a mindset is bring what you have a moment, you are not to saying a good thing what you have a mindset is bring to have what you have a words for wife.

When you have what you have a mindset you can not to be expected to have what you want to have a desire, you are aligned the wrong mindset what you have a mindset to change the way to talk with your wife, you are believing your subconscious mind and you are to saying what you are saying.

You can not to get a good thought from your wife, you are to thinking again form what you have a mindset, you are to change what you have energy what you have a mindset is taking your energy and to give you to be drain in your moment.

You cannot forward for what you want to have a desire; you are aligned the wrong mindset when you are aligned what you are aligned mindset you are strength what you have a realty this you have a realty is not to give what you want to have.

You are unconscious for your right mindset, you are now conscious in your conscious mind is your wrong mindset when you are conscious what you are conscious is your wrong mindset you can not to change what you have a realty you are believing what you have a mindset.

When you are believe, what you have mindset; you are to go backward for what you want to have a desire, you are congruent the wrong mindset what you are congruent mindset can not to created a good thought for your wife.

To get what you want to get your desire for your wife ; you need to change what you have a mindset when you are living in your wrong mindset you are giving your focus for what you have a wrong mindset, focusing in your conscious mind is your wrong mindset to produce more what you have a wrong thought so, you need to be living in a different mindset if you want to break what you have a mindset, when you are living in a different mindset what you have a mindset is your right mindset, you are now conscious in your conscious mind is your right mindset you are to start to change what you have a realty and to have what you want to have a desire.

Your subconscious minds not help you; you have a desire to have a silent moment with yourself, you are now to living in the wrong mindset, your subconscious mind to memorized something and you are to have what you have a mindset, when you have what you have a mindset you are not to get what you want to get your silent moment instead you are upset by what you have a moment, you are conscious in your conscious mind is you wrong mindset.

What you are conscious in your conscious mind is to change the way you feel, you are to be disturb by what you have a mindset what you have a mindset to give you not to get a rest, and you are to go backward for what you want to have a silent moment.

When you are aligned what you are aligned mindset, you can not to get what you want to get you are unconscious for the right mindset, when you are unconscious for your right mindset and you are conscious in your conscious mind is your wrong mindset.

You are to be keeping to go backward for what you want to have a silent moment; you are not conscious the right mindset, you are most of time is to conscious your wrong mindset when you are giving your focus for the wrong mindset you are to strength what you have a realty that what you have a realty not to give you a peaceful moment.

You are competent in your conscious mind is your wrong mindset ; when you are competent for your wrong mindset you are to generated more to distracted what you have a moment, you can not to be expected from what you have a mindset to have what you want to have a silent moment.

To get what you want to get a peaceful moment ; you need to be the right mindset, you are not living in the right mindset what you have a mindset is the wrong mindset when you are most of time to aligned the wrong mindset you are to activating what you are activating realty.

So, you need to break what you have a mindset, if you want to have what you want to have a silent moment ; moving in a different mindset, you are not living in your wrong mindset you are now moving in a different mindset what you have a mindset is your right mindset you can not to have what you had before, you are not focusing in the wrong mindset you are now focusing in your conscious mind is your right mindset what you have a mindset to bring for to have what you want to have a peaceful moment with your time.

10

YOUR SUBCONSCIOUS MIND FOR SPORT

YOUR SUBCONSCIOUS MINDS NOT HELP you; you want to do the sport but your subconscious mind is processing a different mindset, you are now living in a different mindset what you have a mindset to give you to be excused for your sport

You are victims of your subconscious mind; when you are living what you are living mindset, you can not to get what you want to get, you are conscious in your conscious mind is the wrong mindset, you are congruent what you are congruent mindset is a different mindset.

You are to go backward for what you want to do; what you have a mindset is to be a blame mindset, you are not to do what you want to do you are aligned the wrong mindset you are now focusing in your conscious mind is your wrong mindset.

You can not to manifested what you want to manifested ; you are living in the different mindset, what you have a blame mindset to focus, you can to activated what you have a mindset you are now to think from what you have a mindset you can to have what you have a low energy.

When you are keeping what you are keeping mindset; you are to keep to go forward for what you do not want to have, you can not to be expected from what you have a mindset to have what you want to have, what you have a mindset to give you a different attitude that to bring a resisting for what you want to do for sport.

To do what you want to do sport; you need to be, to have the right mindset, you are not living in the right mindset what you have a mindset is coming from your subconscious mind, to have a different mindset.

You are living most of time in your wrong mindset, when you are conscious what you have a mindset in your conscious mind you can not to get the right attitude for your sport, what you have a mindset to created a excused and to have what you have a attitude that what you have attitude is the wrong attitude for sport.

To go forward for your sport; you have to be living in your right mindset, when you are excused for what you want to do sport, you cannot to manifested what you want to manifested, what you are aligned mindset is the wrong mindset, when you are aligned what you are aligned mindset you are focusing in the wrong mind that you are focusing mindset to magnetized a different realty.

So, you need to break what you have a mindset; when you are living the wrong mindset you can to keep what you are manifested but moving in a different mindset what you are moving mindset is the right mindset, you can not to get what you get before, you are to go forward for your sport what you have a mindset is created for you to have what you want to have for sport.

Your subconscious mind not help you, you are not to living in your right mindset when you are in the sport, you are condition into your subconscious mind what you have a mindset to distracted your sport when you are staying unconsciously in your conscious mind is your wrong mindset to change your energy level.

You are victims of your subconscious mind; what you have a mindset is the wrong mindset, when you are aligned the wrong mindset you are feeding your energy for what you have a mindset you can not to have a good attitude for your sport.

You are distracted by what you have a mindset, you are now conscious in your conscious mind is the wrong mindset you are to leak your energy for wrong mindset, you are to go backward for what you want to have for your sport.

You are resisting for what you want to do sport, when you are resisting you are to be living in the wrong mindset, what you have a mindset to give you, to feel the way you are felling for what you want to do sport, you can not to change what you are feeling for your sport.

You are in the wrong mindset; you are unconscious for your mindset, when you are unconscious for your mindset you can not to change the way you are feeling for your sport, you are anchoring by what you have a mindset, when you are anchoring what you are anchoring mindset you can not to change the way you are feeling for your sport.

You are to go backward for what you want to do sport; you are living most of time in your conscious mind is the wrong mindset, what you have a wrong mindset to distract what you want to manifested for sport.

You are unaware your right mindset ; you can to keep what you have a mindset that to bring for you to be staying where you are now, to go forward for your what you want to have for your sport, you need to be living in the right mindset.

When you are moving in your right mindset you can not to get what you have a realty, you are not aligned what you are aligned mindset, you are focusing in your conscious mind is the your right mindset, you are not to focus in your conscious mind is your wrong mindset, you can to break what you have a realty, what you have a mindset is your right mindset you are now most of time focusing in your conscious mind is your right mindset this you have a mindset not to give what you have attitude for your sport you are now living in your right mindset, the mindset you have to bring the right attitude for what you want to do sport and to magnetized what you want to have.

Your subconscious minds not help you; you want to go sport but what you have a mindset to distracted you, you are now living in your wrong mindset, your subconscious mind is condition for something that you are condition of mindset is the wrong mindset, you are now you do not want to go outside form your home, you want to stay into what you have a mindset.

You are victims of your subconscious mind; you are

not living in the right mindset what you have a mindset is the wrong mindset when you are conscious what you are conscious mind in your conscious mind is the wrong mindset.

You can not to have a good feeling form what you have a mindset, what you have a mindset to distracted what you want to do sport, you cannot to have a good self- esteem from what you have a mindset for what you want to do sport.

You are to go backward for what you want to do sport; you are aligned the wrong mindset, when you are aligned what you are aligned you are now focusing in your conscious mind is the wrong mindset you are to be manifested what you do not want to have.

To go forward for what you want to have in your sport; you need to be aware your right mindset, what you have a mindset is taking your energy, you are disturb by what you have a mindset, you do not to have a fun.

What you are conscious in your conscious mind is the wrong mindset, when you are conscious what you are conscious mindset you can not to get a good feeling you are living in a negative mindset this you have a mindset to drain your moment.

You can not to go forward by what you have a mindset; what you have a mindset, to give you to be paralyzed for what you want to do sport, when you live in your wrong mindset you can not to have a good energy instead what you have a mindset to drain your power and to have what you have a bad moment.

To go forward for what you want to do sport ; you need to be living in the right mindset, when you have what you have a mindset you can not to be expected to change what you have energy, you are focusing in your conscious mind is the wrong mindset, to get what you want to get for your sport you need to be aware your right mindset, when you are aware your right mindset you can to start to recognized the wrong mindset, you are now not to focusing in your wrong mindset you are moving is a different mindset what you have a mindset is your right mindset to break what you have energy and to go forward for what you want to do sport.

Your subconscious minds not help you; you are not to be in the right mindset, you are distracted by your subconscious mind what you have a mindset is coming from your subconscious mind process, you are resisting into what you want to do sport, you are in the wrong mindset what you have a mindset to pick your friend criticized and to have a resisting into what you want to do sport.

You are victims of your subconscious mind ; you are not living in the right mindset, what you have a mindset is the wrong mindset, when you are congruent what you are congruent mindset you can not to have what you want to have that you have a mindset to have a different pattern.

You are now living in your subjective mindset ; when you are living what you are living mindset you can to created a belief system, you can say for yourself, he said right, I can not to do that, I am old and other you are to be against for what you want to do sport.

You are to go backward for what you want to do sport; you are living in the wrong mindset what you have a mindset to distract not to do what you want to do sport, if you are keeping what you are keeping mindset.

You are conscious in your conscious mind is your wrong

mindset, you can not to change what you have a realty what you have a mindset is your wrong mindset, you are conscious most of time in your conscious mind is the wrong mindset.

You cannot move forward for what you want to do sport; you are aligned the wrong mindset when you are aligned what you are aligned mindset you can to keep to magnetized what you are magnetized realty.

To get what you want to get for your sport; you need to be know your right mindset, you are now living in your wrong mindset when you live in the wrong mindset you cannot to have a good attitude what you have a resisting attitude to anchor you to stay where you are now.

So, you need to be living in your right mindset ; when you know your right mindset, you are aligned your right mindset you are now conscious in your conscious mind is the right mindset, you are not moving the wrong mindset you are most of time to live in your right mindset, you can not to get what you get before, you are now living in your right mindset what you have a mindset to break what you have a realty, you are conscious in your conscious mind most of time is the right mindset, what you have a mindset to created for you to go forward into what you want to have in your sport.

Your subconscious minds not help you ; you are not doing what you want to do, you are distracted by what you have a mindset this you have a mindset is coming from your subconscious process, you can not to have a good mindset you are going in ritual mindset you are now to live in your wrong mindset.

You are victims of your subconscious of mind; you

can not to go forward for what you want to do, you are aligned yourself for daily ritual mindset this you have a mindset to nagging you, you are to control by what you have a mindset.

You are conscious in your conscious mind is the wrong mindset, when you are conscious what you are conscious mind you can to created a bad day and not to do what you want to do sport, you are aligned the wrong.

What you are aligned the mindset can to give you what you have a realty, you can not to be expected from what you have a mindset to have a different realty instead what you have a mindset is to give you to be saying where you are, you can to go backward for what you want to do sport.

To get what you want to get; you need to be to know what you are congruent mindset, when you are congruent what you are congruent mindset what you are congruent mindset is the wrong mindset you can not to shift what you have energy form what you have a mindset, when you are staying into what you have energy you can to keep what you have a bad day and to go backward for what you want to do sport.

Your energy level anchored by what you have a mindset ; when you are staying most of time you can to have what you have more, when you have what you have you can distracted your day and not to have what you want to have in your sport.

You are conscious most of time in your conscious mind is the wrong mindset, what you have focus the wrong mindset when you are focusing in your conscious mind is the wrong mindset you are feeding your energy for wrong mindset, you can not to be expected to have what you want to have in your sport.

To get what you want to get; you need to be breaking what you have a mindset, when you are moving in the different mindset you can not to get what you have a realty, you are now moving is a different mindset this you have a mindset is your right mindset, to break what you have energy level, you are now conscious in your conscious mind is your right mindset, you can to have what you want to have what you have a mindset to magnetized what you want to have for the sport.

Printed in the United States
By Bookmasters